The Christian,
The Church,
And
Contemporary
Problems

by T. B. MASTON

WORD BOOKS, Publishers
Waco, Texas–London, England

00641

Grateful acknowledgment is made to the following for permission to use copyright material:

THE MOODY BIBLE INSTITUTE
Quotations from *The New Testament In The Language Of The People*, by Charles B. Williams. Copyright 1937, 1949, 1967.

CAMBRIDGE UNIVERSITY PRESS
Quotations from *The New English Bible, New Testament*, Copyright by The Delegates of the Oxford University Press and the Syndics of the Cambridge University Press, 1961. Used by permission.

THE MACMILLAN COMPANY
Quotations from *The New Testament in Modern English* by J. B. Phillips. Copyright 1947, 1952, 1955, 1957, 1958. Used by permission.

THE DIVISION OF CHRISTIAN EDUCATION OF THE NATIONAL COUNCIL OF THE CHURCHES OF CHRIST
Quotations from *The Revised Standard Version of the Bible*. Copyright © 1946 and 1952.

THE LOCKMAN FOUNDATION
Quotations from the *New American Standard Bible, New Testament*. Copyright 1960, 1962, 1963.

ZONDERVAN PUBLISHING HOUSE
Quotations from *The Amplified Bible*. Copyright 1954, 1958, 1962, 1964, 1965.

HARPER AND ROW PUBLISHERS, INC.
Quotations from *A New Translation of the Bible* by James Moffatt. Copyright 1922, 1924, 1926, 1935.

Library of Congress Catalog Card Number: 68-23116

Printed in the United States of America

Preface

We become Christians through union with the resurrected Christ. This experience brings us into the family of God. The more we mature in our understanding of God and of His way in our lives and in the world, the more we realize that the Christian life is as broad and as deep as life itself. There is enough in the Christian life to challenge us to the end of life's journey.

This continuing challenge stems, to some degree, from the fact that the God we worship and serve is the sovereign God of the universe. As sovereign He is interested in and concerned about the totality of the life of the individual and of the world. He may have a unique concern for some aspects of life but He cannot be restricted to any one segment of life.

The more thoroughly we are acquainted with the basic teachings of the Scriptures, the more we will see that God expects His children to be like Him. This means, among other things, that His children are to be interested in the totality of life. In turn, this means that no individual, regardless of creed, class, culture, or color, should be outside of our genuine concern. It also means that we should be concerned not merely for their "souls" but for them as persons. Furthermore, we should be interested in and concerned for the total life of the world: our nation and its people, but also other nations of the world and their people.

It has been a personal conviction for many years that the out-standing weakness of contemporary Christianity is the ethical or moral weakness. Our preaching is better than our practice. This weakness seems to be particularly evident in churches and Chris-tian groups that major on "evangelism" and who pride themselves on their theological conservatism. It may be that the words of Jesus, spoken in another context, would be applicable to many of us and to our churches: "These you ought to have done, without neglecting the others" (Matt. 23:23, RSV). As is so frequently true, the choice is not an either/or but a both/and. Let us con-tinue our emphasis on bringing men into union with Christ, but let us help them to mature in their comprehension of what this union with Christ means in daily life. It means basically to be like Him, and let us never forget that He went about doing good (Acts 10:38): feeding the hungry, ministering to the social and moral outcasts of His day, lifting the downtrodden, healing the afflicted, and forgiving the sinful.

The chapters in the present volume seek to apply the Chris-tian message and spirit to contemporary social and moral prob-lems. They were originally articles or addresses. An attempt has been made to organize them logically and give to them an under-lying unity.

There are four chapters gathered together in Part One that attempt to set forth some basic concepts which underline or undergird the Christian concern for people and for the world in which they live. Part Two is devoted to family problems; Part Three to racial problems; and Part Four to political problems, with the last chapter in Part Four discussing the contemporary world crisis.

A considerable biblical flavor is maintained throughout the chapters with this emphasis particularly evident in Part One. This is done with the conviction that a Christian concern for the world and its problems not only stems from the nature of God but also from the nature of the biblical revelation in general.

The fact that this book is a collection of articles and addresses written by request over a period of time helps to explain certain limitations. The careful reader will know that some problems are touched on very lightly, if at all.

A word of appreciation should be expressed to those who originally extended the invitations to write an article or to make an address. Chapter 9 is a revision and an abridgment of a chapter in my *Segregation and Desegregation,* published by the Macmillan Company in 1959, a book that is now out of print. Chapter 15 has been reproduced from *Chapel Messages* (Baker, 1966), edited by H. C. Brown, Jr., and Charles B. Johnson, and is included in this volume by the courtesy of Baker Book House.

It is hoped that those who read these chapters will grasp more clearly the breadth and depth of our Christian faith. It is our prayer that at least some of those who read them will be led to commit themselves more fully to the purposes of God in the world.

T. B. MASTON

Unless otherwise indicated all quotations of the Scriptures are from the Revised Standard Version. Abbreviations are used for some of the other translations, such as NEB for the New English Bible, NASB for the New American Standard Bible, and Williams (Charles B.) and Phillips for their translations of the New Testament.

Contents

Contents

Part I

BASIC CONCEPTS

The four chapters in Part I offer an introduction to, or supply a background for, the remaining chapters of the book. Logically, we begin with a chapter on the Bible. This is followed with a chapter on the close relation of theology and ethics, a relationship that is evident throughout the Bible. The movement from these two chapters is rather natural to the relation of the Christian and the Christian church to the world. These four chapters provide, to a large degree, a justification or a rationale for Christian concern for the world and the peoples of the world.

Chapter 1

THE BIBLICAL BASIS FOR SOCIAL CONCERN

One definition of religion is that it is what one does with his solitariness. There is an element of truth in this statement. The central core of the Christian faith is a face-to-face encounter of man with God. This is a strictly personal matter, but it is not a purely private matter. The Christian's encounter with God does not and cannot remain entirely private. The person who has been brought face to face with God plays certain roles in society. He maintains certain relations in the home, in the church, in the workaday world, and society in general. If his encounter with God is meaningful, it will affect every role he plays, every relation he maintains. In other words, it will carry over into life.

This "carry over into life" stems, to a considerable degree, from the nature of the God with whom the individual has been brought face to face. The Bible plainly reveals that God, the creator and sovereign ruler of the universe, is concerned with the *totality* of life. The same will be true of His children if their relation to Him is vital enough for them to have captured or been captured by His spirit. This means that there is an important and even an inevitable place in the Christian's life, from the biblical perspective, for a concern for the world and its problems and for the peoples of the world.

13

A COVENANT PEOPLE

One cannot understand properly the biblical basis for social concern unless he understands that the people of God are a covenant people, an idea that pervades the entire Bible. The concept is specifically stated more frequently, however, in the Old Testament. The word *berith* (covenant) is found in approximately three-fourths of the books of the Old Testament.[1] The word *berith* was used by the Israelites and others to describe different types of contracts or agreements: between individuals (Gen. 21:27; 26:28), including husband and wife (Mal. 2:14) and between nations (Ex. 23:32), or the kings or leaders of those nations (1 Kings 20:34; 2 Kings 11:4). However, the word is used, in the main, in the Scriptures to refer to God's covenant with His people. The Scriptures reveal that He was the initiator of the covenant. He stated the conditions that must be agreed to by the people for them to enter into covenant with Him. He promised to bless them provided they would accept the obligations that the covenant entailed.

God entered into covenant with Noah (Gen. 9) and with Abraham (Gen. 17) and possibly with Israel at Moab (Deut. 29), if this was not simply a renewal of His earlier covenant at Mt. Horeb or Sinai. The latter was the major covenant of God with His people. There at Sinai the conditions of the covenant were fully stated in what is usually called "The Book of the Covenant" (Ex. 20:22-23:33).

Introductory to "The Book" or an integral part of it, depending on one's perspective, are the Ten Commandments. They are called "the tables of the testimony" (Ex. 31:18; 32:15; 34:29), or "the tables of the covenant" (Deut. 9:9, 11, 15). They epitomize God's expectations of His covenant people. As the best illustration of apodictic law, a kind of law which states basic principles or operates in the area of categorical imperatives, the commandments are abidingly relevant and applicable.[2]

The Ten Commandments, as is true of apodictic laws in general and also casuistic laws, place obligations on God's people to be right in their relation to Him, to one another and to their fellowmen in general. In other words, in the covenant relationship there is operative the obligation of obedience and also the motive of gratitude—gratitude for what God has done and promises to do for His people. These motives are seen in the introduction to the Ten Commandments: "I am the Lord your God, who brought you out of the land of Egypt, out of the house of bondage" (Ex. 20:2). Because of what He had done, He had a right to command. Also because of what He had done, His people in gratitude should respond to Him. Significant for our purpose is the fact that these commandments express concern for the family, for the sacredness of human life, for the inviolability of the relation of husband and wife, for property, and for the good name of one's neighbor.

The covenant idea is not as frequently and specifically mentioned in the prophets as in the law, yet exhortations regarding social concern are as prevalent in the prophets as in the books of the law. These exhortations are particularly evident in the great eighth century prophets. For example, Isaiah stated that God was not pleased with the offerings of the children of Israel and with their observance of special days and that He would not hear their prayers. He then revealed to them what they must do. To be acceptable to God, they must cleanse their hands:

> cease to do evil, learn to do good;
> seek justice, correct oppression;
> defend the fatherless, plead for the widow.
> (Isa. 1:16,17)

Amos sums up God's expectations as follows:

> But let justice roll down like waters,
> and righteousness like an ever-flowing stream.
> (Amos 5:24)

Micah, in as great a summary statement of the requirements of revealed religion as is found in the Old Testament, says:

> He has showed you, O man, what is good;
> and what does the Lord require of you
> but to do justice, and to love kindness,
> and to walk humbly with your God?
> (Mic. 6:8)

Justice, righteousness, and kindness operate in the area of social concern. They are involved in one's relations to the world and the peoples of the world.

The covenant concept or idea is prevalent in the New Testament or Covenant, although the word "covenant" is not found very much except in the Book of Hebrews. It is true that Jesus, when He instituted the Lord's Supper, in referring to the cup, said, "This is my blood of the covenant" (Matt. 26:28; cf. 1 Cor. 11:25; Ex. 24:8). This was the new covenant spoken of by Jeremiah (31:31-34) and by the author of Hebrews (8:6-13).

In this new covenant Christians are the new Israel. They are the people of God, and He has entered into covenant with them. This is a new and better covenant. It is better because it "is inward or spiritual; it is individual and therefore universal; it is gracious and provides forgiveness."[3] The new covenant is a work of grace, yet the response of faith to that grace involves obedience to the One who is the source of the grace. We are "God's handiwork" created in Christ Jesus, but created "to devote ourselves to the good deeds for which God has designed us" (Eph. 2:10, NEB).

THE CHRISTIAN COMMUNITY

The Christian's social concern should express itself in an unusual way within the Christian community or fellowship (koinonia). This fellowship is drawn together and held together by the common experience in the Lord of the members and by their love for Him. There was a depth of fellowship in the Jerusalem church that has seldom been duplicated. Their fellowship was so meaningful that they shared with one another in a way and to a degree that has perplexed and at times frustrated some of the followers of Christ through the years.

The record says that they "had all things in common *[koina]*; and they sold ["continued to sell," Williams] their possessions and goods and distributed them to all as any had need ["as anyone had special need." Williams] (Acts 2:44-45). Because they shared so freely with one another, "there was not a needy person among them" (Acts 4:34). No wonder the apostles could bear "witness with great power to the resurrection of the Lord Jesus," and that "they were all held in high esteem" (Acts 4:33, NEB).

It should be remembered that the sharing in the Jerusalem Christian community resulted from the fact that those within the community "devoted themselves to . . . fellowship *[koinonia]*" (Acts 2:42), and "were of one heart and soul" (Acts 4:32). Their sharing was an outer manifestation of their inner unity. Actually, there is inherent in the idea of Christian fellowship or *koinonia* the idea of sharing. Paul used the word *koinonia* on at least three occasions to refer to the collection for the saints at Jerusalem (Rom. 15:26; 2 Cor. 8:4; 9:13).

The expression of concern for those within the Christian community is particularly prominent in the epistles of Paul and John, both of whom wrote primarily to and for Christians. Paul's concern stemmed, to a considerable degree, from his conception of the church. His favorite figure or image for the Christian fellowship was the body of Christ *[soma christou]*, with Christ as the head (see 1 Cor. 12 and Eph. 4). The unity within the body is underscored by the fact that Paul's conception of the body was primarily if not exclusively Hebraic rather than Hellenic—the body for him referred to the whole person rather than exclusively to the physical body. There are many parts but one body (1 Cor. 10:17; 12:20). These parts are so closely knit together that if one member suffers, they all suffer (1 Cor. 12:26). Right for a member of the body is to be determined largely by the effect of one's actions on the body and on the other members of the body. For example, if eating meat offered to idols offends, makes weak, or causes a weaker brother to stumble, the member of the body is to eat no more meat (1 Cor. 8; Rom. 14). Within the fellowship one should not seek his own good ["interests," NEB; "advantage," Phillips; "welfare," Williams] but the good of his neighbor (1 Cor. 10:24). He should give no offense to the Jews, the Greeks, or the church of God (1 Cor. 10:32).

Paul's admonition is: "Let all things be done for ["with a view to"⁴] edification" (1 Cor. 14:26). Within the Christian fellowship there is to be "no provoking of one another, no envy of one another" (Gal. 5:26), or as Williams translates it, "Let us stop being ambitious for honors, so challenging one another, envying one another." The members are to "bear one another's burdens [burdens "about to press one down"⁵], and so fulfill the law of Christ" (Gal. 6:2). Williams, as he typically does, brings out the verb tense in this verse as follows: "Practice bearing one another's burdens, and in this way carry out the law of Christ," possibly referring to the law of love, the Master's "new commandment" (John 13:34).

Paul's concern for the Christian community is spelled out in a special way in his use of love [agape]. Most of his references to agape are within the context of the Christian community, including his great love chapter which was written to the church at Corinth. In this same letter he suggests that knowledge puffs up, "makes arrogant" (NASB), or "breeds conceit" (NEB), but love edifies or builds up (1 Cor. 8:1)—"Love is the solution, not knowledge, in all social problems."⁶ To the Thessalonians Paul says, "But concerning love of the brethren [philadelphias] you have no need to have anyone write to you." Why is this true? He gives the answer as follows: "For you yourselves have been taught by God to love [agapan] one another." He follows this with a statement and an exhortation. The statement is, "Indeed you do love all the brethren throughout Macedonia," and the exhortation is, "But we exhort you, brethren, to do so more and more" ["to excel still more," NASB] (1 Thess. 4:9-10). The Colossians are admonished to forbear "one another" and forgive "one another." Then over these and all other qualities that should characterize "God's chosen ones ["his own, his beloved," NEB]," they should put on love "which binds everything together in perfect harmony" (Col. 3:14), or "which is the perfect bond of unity" (NASB)—binds the virtues together, or possibly better, binds those within the Christian fellowship together.

As previously suggested, John, particularly in 1 John, expresses a comparable concern for those within the Christian community. Similar to Paul, his use of *agape* (love) is largely restricted to the Christian fellowship. Love for the brethren is both a motive for concern for them and an integral part of that concern. The source of this love is God. In its deepest and truest sense love or *agape* is the spontaneous fruit of a vital relationship with God who is *agape*—*agape* is the very essence of His being. John says that "we know that we have passed out of death into life ["have crossed the frontier from death to life," Phillips], because we love the brethren" (1 John 3:14)—"proof of this transition, not the ground of it." [7] One who does not love, does not know ["never knew" [8]] God since God is love (1 John 4:8). Also, since God is love, one "who abides ["dwells," NEB] in love abides in God ["continues in union with God," Williams; "is dwelling in God," NEB] and God abides in him" (4:16)— "the nature of the believer must be conformed to the Nature of God." [9] John also says, "We love because he first loved us" (4:19)—"the amazing love of God in Christ is the inspiration of all the love that stirs in our hearts."[10] Love characterizes our lives because He first loved us—"Our love is the light kindled by the love of God." [11] Our response to His love for us is not only in our love for Him; we also make ourselves channels for His love for others. Or, as John says, if God loved us enough to give His Son as the propitiation, sacrifice, or remedy for our sins "we also ought to love ["keep on loving" [12]] one another" (4:11). Again he says that Christ laid down His life for us and "we ought to lay down our lives for the brethren" (3:16). He also says, "Whoever loves the Father loves the child born of Him"

(5:1, NASB), or literally, "Whoever loves the one who begets, loves the begotten" (see marg. in NASB). "Love for God is the inner principle, love for the brethren its outward manifestation." [13]

John applies the great principle of love in a specific way in at least one place. He says: "But if anyone has the world's goods and sees ["deliberately contemplates" [14]] his brother in need, yet closes his heart against him ["slamming the door of his compassion" [15]], how does God's love abide in him?" (3:17). Notice that he does not say, "How does love of his brother abide in him," but rather, "How does God's love abide in him?" This is not our love for God, but God's love as expressed in and through us.

THE COMMUNITY OF THE WORLD

The children of God are our spiritual brothers but included in this group may be neighbors and friends of all classes and races. Also, those in the community of the world who are not in the Christian family are our potential brothers in Christ. Furthermore, the effectiveness with which we reach them for Christ will be determined, to a considerable degree, by whether or not we treat them like brothers. Really, the Christian's love and concern must and will inevitably overflow the boundaries of the Christian community and reach out to the community of the world. This outreach is emphasized in both the Old and New Testaments. For example, it is revealed in the Old Testament that God was not only the God of Israel, but that He was also the God of all the nations. His ultimate purpose was that the words of the Lord should go out to all nations (Isa. 2:2-3; Mic. 4:1-2).

The word of the resurrected Christ to His disciples was that they were to go and make and baptize disciples or learners of all the nations. They were also to teach them to obey all that He had commanded them (Matt. 28:18-20)—"The teaching is with a view not to *gnosis* but to practice; the aim is not orthodox opinion but right living." [16] They were to be witnesses not only in Jerusalem and Judea but also in hated Samaria and to the end or "remotest part" (NASB) of the earth (Acts 1:8). It was an inclusive commission, being in harmony with the general emphasis of His teachings. He never placed any limits on any of His basic teachings. They may have been directed immediately to the disciples, but the disciples in turn were to apply them to the world community. His disciples were to be "the salt of the earth," "the light of the world." They should so shine their light before men that they might see their good works and give glory to their Father who was in heaven (Matt. 5:13-16)—"The noble works which glorify the Father reveal the workers to be sons." [17] He taught them to pray:

> Thy kingdom come,
> Thy will be done,
> On earth as it is in heaven.
> (Matt. 6:10)

What they prayed for, they were also to work and live for.

They were to love their neighbor as themselves (Matt. 22:39; cf. Lev. 19:18). Their neighbor was anyone in need (see Luke 10:25-37). They were even to love ["practice loving," Williams] their enemies and to pray for those who persecuted them (Matt. 5:44). If they loved only those who loved them, they would do no more than the despised tax collector, and if they saluted or greeted only their brethren, they would not do anything more than others—even the Gentiles ["heathen," NEB] (Matt. 5:46-47). Christ did not and does not want His disciples to be "moral mediocrities, men of average morality, but to be morally superior, uncommon." [18]

While Paul was concerned primarily with the Christian community, he did have a considerable place for the world community in his teachings. To the Galatians he said: "As we have opportunity, let us do good ["practice doing good," Williams] to all men," and then added, "and especially to those who are of the household of faith" (Gal. 6:10). He admonished the Thessalonians to "increase and abound ["mount and overflow," NEB] in love to one another and to all men" (1 Thess. 3:12). Here the inclusive "all men" comes as a climax (cf. 2 Pet. 1:5-8). He also told the Thessalonians that they should so live as to "command the respect of outsiders" (1 Thess. 4:12). He says that he aims "at what is honorable not only in the Lord's sight but also in the sight of men" (2 Cor. 8:21). He exhorted the Romans to "take thought for what is noble in the sight of all" (Rom. 12:17), or "respect what is right in the sight of all men" (NASB). The Philippians were to "shine as lights in the world" (Phil. 2:15), while the Colossians were to conduct themselves "wisely toward outsiders" (Col. 4:5) or those outside the church. Even a hungry, thirsty enemy was to have his needs provided (Rom. 12:20).

The members of the Christian community were to be subject to "governing authorities" because such authorities were ordained or "instituted by God," and to resist them was to resist God (Rom. 13:1-2). This subjection to the state as to other human institutions should be, to use a Petrine expression, "for the Lord's sake" (1 Pet. 2:13). The implication is that there are limits to the subjection or obedience due to representatives of any human institution. This subjection is not justified when the Lord's cause would not be served, or when the governing authorities or human institutions are no longer within the purposes of God. At such a time, the voice of the child of God and even of the Christian community should be "we must obey God rather than men" (Acts 5:29; cf. Acts 4:17). After all, Christians should only render unto Caesar what belongs to him, and supreme loyalty and devotion belong to God (see Mark 12:13-17).

What has been said may be summarized by saying that for the Christian and the Christian community *there can be no retreat from the world.* God has not seceded from history; His people are to cooperate with Him in the making of history. He is in a continuing struggle to extend His sovereignty, His rule, His reign, His kingdom in the world. His people are to be laborers together with Him in His work in the world. G. Ernest Wright claims that "in the New Testament . . . we have much more material dealing with the responsibility of the community of Christ to its Lord *before* the world than we have of an active responsibility for the salvation of the world." [19] He suggests that this is true because salvation is in the hands of God. It is also possible that this is true because the most effective thing children of God can do to bring others to salvation in Christ is to be consistent living witnesses of the grace of God as that grace finds expression in every area of their lives.

THE KINSHIP MOTIVE

This study would not be complete without a brief statement concerning the kinship motive as a basis for social concern. There have been suggested, without spelling them out in detail, at least three grounds or motives for such concern: obedience, gratitude, and love. In turn, the main ground for these motives is the fact that we are a covenant people. There has been outlined, in an admittedly brief and inadequate way, the working of these motives in two major areas: within the Christian community and in the community of the world. The kinship motive likewise is operative in both of these areas.

The kinship idea is prevalent in both testaments. God has always wanted His people to be like Him. The children of Israel were to be kind and helpful to the fatherless, the widow, and the stranger or sojourner in their midst. There were two reasons why this should be true: (1) God is just in His dealings with these "His special protégés"—His people should likewise treat them justly, and (2) the Israelites should remember that they were sojourners in Egypt and God delivered them (see Deut. 10:18-19; 24:17). Here is both the kinship motive and the gratitude motive. There are places where God specifically says that His people are to be like Him. For example, He says, "You shall be holy; for I the Lord your God am holy" (Lev. 19:2; cf. 11:44). The same could be said concerning every quality and attribute of God. These qualities or attributes of God, if they can properly be called attributes, were and are expressed in His concern for and His dealings with people. The acts of God in relationship to His people and to the nations of the world reveal His character. God's people are to reveal their kinship to Him by the way they treat those about them.

The appeal for kinship to God is clearly seen in the New Testament. For example, Jesus appealed to His disciples to love their enemies, and gave as the reason or motive that they might be sons of their Father "for he makes his sun rise on the evil and on the good, and sends rain on the just and on the unjust." He closed this great statement or appeal with the continually challenging words: "You, therefore, must be perfect, as your heavenly Father is perfect" (Matt. 5:43-48). The words that give this statement its greatest depth and challenge are: "as your heavenly Father." His children are to be like him.

Paul's appeal to the Philippians was, "Have this attitude in yourselves which was also in Christ Jesus" (Phil. 2:5, NASB). The appeal, at this particular point, was to humility. He says Christ "emptied himself, humbled himself and became obedient unto death." Paul also said that Christ set the example for His followers in regard to love. To the Ephesians he wrote: "Walk [peripateo—literally "walk around," "practice living," Williams] in love, as Christ loved us and gave himself up for us" (Eph. 5:2). He appealed to the Corinthians to be imitators of him as he was of Christ (1 Cor. 11:1; cf. 1 Thess. 1:6). He exhorted the Colossians to forgive one another as the Lord had forgiven them (Col. 3:13; cf. Eph. 4:32). He used the example of Jesus to appeal for a liberal offering for the saints at Jerusalem (2 Cor. 8:1-9). He concludes the argument concerning the eating of meat offered to idols as follows: "We who are strong ought to bear with the failings of the weak, and not to please ourselves; let each of us please his neighbor for his good, to edify him." Why should this be true? Paul gives the answer as follows: "For Christ did not please himself; but, as it is written, 'The reproaches of those who reproached thee fell on me.'" (Rom. 15:1-3).

The initial invitation of Jesus was: "Follow me" (Mark 1:17; 2:14; Matt. 4:19; 9:9). It was repeated at Caesarea Philippi (Matt. 16:24) and to the rich young ruler (Mark 10:21; Matt. 19:21). It is the initial and continuing invitation of Jesus to His disciples in every age. To be a Christian is to walk in the way that He walked. He did not and does not give detailed instructions about that way. The best instructions come from examining the life He lived. His life as well as His teachings provide, however, a compass rather than a road map. That compass points to the open road of a deepening fellowship with Him as we seek to go about doing good (see Acts 10:38), as we express something of His compassion for people—for sinning, suffering individuals (Luke 7:13), as well as for the struggling, restless masses who are harassed and helpless, like sheep without a shepherd (Matt. 9:36; cf. 14:14; 15:32).

We can be assured as we walk in His way that it is not an uncharted course. He has traveled that way before us. How grateful we should be, however, that Jesus has not only traveled that way but that He walks in that way with His disciples now. His word is "I am with you always" (Matt. 28:20). He is not only a pattern of life for us to follow, but a companion to give us strength to walk in the way with Him. Manson expresses beautifully something of the relation of Christ to His follower. He says, "The living Christ still has two hands, one to point the way, and the other held out to help us along." [20] If we follow where He leads, we will seek as best we can to let Him express Himself in us and through us in every relation we have with those without, as well as within, the Christian community. May we be increasingly captured by His concern and compassion for the world and the peoples of the world!

Chapter 2

THE RELATION OF THEOLOGY AND ETHICS

The close relation of theology and ethics is clearly seen in the Law, the Prophets, and the Writings of the Old Testament. It is equally as evident in the teachings of Jesus, the Johannine literature, the Pauline epistles, and the general epistles. Nowhere does the vital relation of the two stand out more clearly than in the Ephesian letter.

The superlatives of the English language have been applied to this relatively brief epistle. Mackay considers it the greatest and maturest of all of Paul's writings,[1] "and for our time, the most relevant of his works."[2] Lidgett contends that it is "the final statement of Pauline theology," and the most comprehensive statement in the New Testament "of the meaning of the Christian religion, blending as nowhere else its evangelical, spiritual, moral, and universal elements."[3] Carver believes that Ephesians is "the supreme monograph of all time,"[4] and "the most comprehensive, the most complete, the most incisive and creative of all the New Testament writings."[5]

ITS TWO DIVISIONS

One of the reasons for the influence of Ephesians is its rather remarkable balancing of theology and ethics. In this epistle, as is true of several of Paul's other epistles, there is a fairly well defined doctrinal or theological portion of the epistle followed by a practical or applied section. Paul usually makes the transition from the more theological to the more practical by the use of the word "therefore." This is a favorite word of his, frequently used to bridge two ideas, or to relate one idea to another. The major transition in Ephesians is at the beginning of chapter four. In words strikingly similar to Romans 12:1 he says: "I therefore . . . beg you ["beseech you," KJV; "entreat you," NEB] to live a life worthy of the calling to which you have been called." The word "therefore" bridges or ties together the doctrinal section of the epistle and the practical, or the applied. The first chapters "lead us to the secrets and resources of the Christian life, and the last to its exercise in the Church and in the world." [6]

This does not mean that theology is not practical; neither does it mean that there is no theology in chapters four through six. While the division is clearly evident, it is primarily a matter of emphasis. It simply represents a transition in Paul's "center of gravity." [7] While theology is not left behind, the last three chapters are, in the main, for exhortation and challenge. It should never be forgotten, however, that with Paul, in the biblical revelation in general and in Christian experience, there is no divorcement of theology and ethics. These are merely two sides of one coin, or the "two sides of one picture," and the two sides represent "the total Christian approach to life." [8] "Christian faith and Christian morals are inseparable," [9] and "the most wonderful mysteries of the Christian revelation have a direct relation to conduct." [10] Theology and ethics, as Carver suggests, "cannot be put asunder without serious results for genuine religion." He adds that "if doctrine is not practical—and practiced—it is unreal, delusive, and useless. If experience and conduct are not integral with truth, they are lacking in meaning and reality." [11]

It should not be forgotten that Paul's basic ethic, in contrast to his applied ethic, is found primarily in the so-called theological sections of some of his major epistles, including Ephesians. This can be plainly seen in the study of "Faith and Works" and "Unity in Christ," two major divisions of this chapter.

Paul was always concerned with the ethical and was never more so "than when he was most profoundly metaphysical." [12] For Paul, "an effective religion must be thoroughly and passionately ethical, and it can be so only if based on sound and secure convictions as to God—theology; and on a realistic understanding of man—anthropology." [13]

FAITH AND WORKS

One evidence, as suggested previously, of the interrelatedness of theology and ethics in the Ephesian letter is seen in the close relation of faith and works. This relationship is implied throughout the epistle. For example, Paul says that he had heard of the faith of the Ephesians "in the Lord Jesus" and their "love toward all the saints" (1:15). In the wonderfully rich passage which closes the more theological portion of the epistle, and in a sense is the climax of the entire epistle, Paul reveals that he prays for the Ephesians that "through faith Christ" might dwell in their hearts "in love." He further prays that they may grasp "with all God's people, what is the breadth and length and height and depth of the love of Christ, and to know it, though it is beyond knowledge" (3:17-19, NEB). It is the love of Christ that is the secret to the Christian's love for the saints as well as the secret to whatever good deeds or good works he may produce.

The close relationship of faith and works is spelled out most specifically in the first few verses of chapter two. The Ephesians are reminded that they, along with others who were once dead in trespasses and sins, have been made alive through their union with Christ. They have been raised "up with Him" (a theme he discusses more fully in Colossians 3), and made to sit "in the heavenly places in Christ Jesus" (2:5-6). Paul sums up the matter by saying, "For by grace you have been saved through faith; and this is not your own doing, it is the gift of God—not because of works, lest any man should boast" (2:8-9). This is an enlargement of his parenthetical statement in verse 5, and is what Bruce calls "one of the great evangelical summaries of the New Testament." [14] Paul makes it very plain that salvation is by grace with faith as the channel for the operation of that grace. It "is not an achievement but a gift." [15]

The faith that saves, however, goes deeper and is more significant than many Christians seem to realize. We have been brought into union with the crucified and resurrected Christ. We are God's workmanship or "masterpiece," created in or through union with Christ Jesus. We are in Christ; He is in us. He is in the vine, we are the branches, "though as yet the leaf has hardly escaped from its sheaf and the flower is only timidly opening itself to the sun and the air." [16] How grateful we ought to be, however, for the unlimited potential in the experience. All that limits us in our growth in, and our service for, Him is our responsiveness to the Spirit's leadership in our lives. Through this experience, which is by grace through faith, there comes into our lives a depth of perception and a breadth of perspective that we had not known before.

One thing that we perceive is that the experience, at least in one sense, is not an end within itself. There is a purpose that goes beyond the immediate experience. This purpose is clearly revealed in the latter part of verse 10. We are created in Christ Jesus for or "with a view to good works," [17] or "to devote ourselves to the good deeds for which God has designed us" (NEB). Good works, or a life of goodness, was the design or purpose of God even while we were yet in our trespasses and sins. The salvation that we have through faith makes it possible for us to fulfill God's design or purpose for our lives. This purpose of God is so central in the experience that it really becomes the proof of the experience. In other words, we prove that we have been saved through faith by the quality of life we live.

One commentator states the matter as follows: "No one more wholeheartedly than Paul repudiated good works as a *ground* of salvation," and yet "no one more wholeheartedly insisted on good

works as the *fruit* of salvation." [18] Another author has referred
to the relation of faith and works as "the Pauline paradox," but
he also says that it is "an inevitable law of love."[19] The grace of
God which is an expression of His love for us has put us in debt
to Him for the remainder of our lives. We try, as best we can,
to prove our gratitude by bearing fruit or producing good works
for Him.

UNITY IN CHRIST

Reconciliation or unity, which is achieved through and in
Christ, is another central emphasis in the epistle. Before we
discuss the subject in a more specific way, let us look briefly at
those two little but tremendously significant words: "in Christ."
If these words are not "the central category of Paul's thinking"[20]
or his "favorite expression,"[21] they are certainly one of the basic
concepts of his thought. The words are found rather frequently
in Ephesians, and the concept permeates the entire epistle. Markus
Barth expresses the pervasiveness of the concept as follows:
"God's eternal will, God's work, and the daily life of the Ephesians
are held together by a oneness, unity, and bond which bears but
one name: Christ."[22]

The expression "in Christ" evidently refers, in most cases, to
a mystical union with Him. To be in Christ is something deeper,
broader, and more meaningful than to be in the Church, "which
is His body." Through union with Christ, the child of God finds
sustenance and strength to live the Christian life. Through the
consciousness of the presence of the indwelling Christ, he is challenged to live a God-centered rather than a self-centered life. In
other words, when one is in Christ, "a new principle of life has
been implanted" within him. His "outlook has been reoriented
towards God."[23] He sees that his life is increasingly to be conformed to the image of the One who lives in Him. He is to learn
Christ (4:20). Christ becomes the soil in which he grows, the
atmosphere he breathes, the source and goal of his entire existence.
He understands more and more clearly that the moral life for the

Christian is not something that is superficial or external. It flows out from within. The fruit of the Christian's life results from his union with Christ. This means, among other things, that the fruit is natural and even inevitable. The more deeply and consistently he lives in Christ, the more abundant will be the fruit he will bear for Christ.

One glorious result of a person's union with Christ is his reconciliation with God and with his fellowman. This reconciliation, which is both vertical and horizontal, is one of the major themes of the letter to the Ephesians. Near the beginning of the epistle Paul says that the purpose of God, "which he set forth in Christ," is "to unite all things in him, things in heaven [vertical] and things on earth [horizontal]" (1:9-10). He also reveals that all things are to be put under Christ's feet and He is to be made "the head over all things" (1:22). "God has constituted Jesus Christ the unifying center of the vast scheme of unity whereby the celestial and terrestrial orders, separated as they now are by the great gulf between the supernatural and the natural, and the greater gulf between the holy and the sinful, shall be joined together in a united Commonwealth."[24] The primary gulf that needs to be crossed, or the barrier that needs to be broken down, is between man and God. It is the enmity between God and man, in the final analysis, that begets enmity among men. This means, among other things, that there is no sound hope for reconciliation between men unless they are reconciled to God. On the other hand, "men cannot be reconciled to God without being also reconciled to one another."[25] Both reconciliations, vertical and horizontal, are effected by Christ and are indissolubly united in Him. This means, among other things, that one who is wrong in his spirit toward people of other races, classes, and cultures cannot be right with God regardless of what he may think or say.

Let us repeat, however, that the horizontal rift between man and man can only be removed in and through Christ. It was Christ and He alone who was able to make Jew and Gentile one. And it should be remembered that "no iron curtain, color bar, class distinction, or national frontier of today is more absolute than the cleavage between the Jew and Gentile was in antiquity."[26] However, in Christ this barrier was broken down, "the dividing wall of hostility" (2:14) was eliminated. "Wall" evidently referred to a wall in the Temple which separated the court of the Gentiles from the other courts in the temple area. Paul also suggests that Christ abolished the law of commandments and ordinances "that he might create in himself one new man in the place of the two ["one new kind of person"[27]], so making peace" (2:15). Notice again the source for such peace among men; it is through the reconciliation of both to God "in one body through the cross, thereby bringing the hostility to an end" (2:16). The only real hope for peace among men is through their oneness in Christ, a oneness that, in turn, is made possible only through the cross. Through union with the crucified and resurrected Christ we become members of the same body (2:16, cf. 3:6) and are brought into the household of God, who is the Father of all who believe and who is no respecter of persons. "The meaning clearly is that God proposes to relate to Himself in one great family people whom historical hates, cultural differences, and social status, have held apart."[28] How relevant for a world torn with racial and class strife! It is Robertson who says, "Race and national distinction vanish in Christ."[29]

Summers suggests that "the different propositions presented and discussed by Paul in this epistle follow one after the other as natural corollaries. The *one* God has provided *one* way of redemption; it is for *all* men without regard to race; it must follow that it makes all men *one* in Christ."[30] Such a oneness in Christ is the great need of the world. The real problem in our world "is to constitute a spiritual unity in which men, being united in their loyalty to God, shall be loyally devoted to one another."[31] This means not a superficial unity but a real community, and "the community which God wills is a fellowship of love, constituted not by an evolution in history, but by the intervention of God in history."[32]

CHRISTIAN MATURITY

Paul was abidingly concerned about the maturity of his converts and his churches. He discusses this matter in a particularly specific way in chapter four of the Ephesian letter, which is, incidentally, the first major passage we have referred to from the so-called practical or applied portion of the epistle.

The author reveals that Christ's gifts were that some should be apostles, prophets, evangelists, pastors, and teachers. He also reveals the purpose or purposes of their special gifts. The overall purpose is "to equip God's people in his service" (4:12, NEB). What a difference a comma may make! For example, the Authorized Version, the American Standard Version, and the Revised Standard Version retain the comma after "saints" which would mean that the purpose of the work of the specially gifted ones was threefold—to equip the saints or God's people, to carry on the work of the ministry, and to build up the body of Christ. This separates the "clergy" from the "laity" in a way which is out of harmony with the New Testament emphasis. In contrast, the New English Bible, Phillips, Weymouth, Williams, and others omit the comma after the word "saints." This would make it mean that the inclusive purpose of the work of the specially gifted ones was to equip the "saints," the rank and file of church members, so the latter, along with those who had been called to perform special functions, would be able to carry on the work of the ministry and thus build up the body of Christ. What a tremendous contribution would be made to the maturity of the churches and their members if the preceding idea were understood and taken seriously by both "ministers" and "laymen."

Paul then spells out more specifically what is the work of the ministry which is the responsibility of all of God's children. The major purpose is the building up of the body of Christ "until we all [those who are called to perform special functions along with all the saints] attain to the unity of the faith and of the knowledge of the Son of God, to mature manhood,

to the measure of the stature of the fullness of Christ ["to a mature manhood and to a perfect measure of Christ's moral stature," Williams]" (4:13). Here is the measure of Christian
maturity. How tall are we when we stand up beside Christ,
when our maturity "is measured by nothing less than the full
stature of Christ" (NEB)? The high demands of our maturity
are inherent in the experience when we come into union with
Christ. Paul says that we are "to grow up in every way into him"
or "into perfect union with Him" (Williams) (v. 15).

We are no longer to be children "tossed to and fro and carried
about with every wind of doctrine, by the cunning of men, by
their craftiness in deceitful wiles" (v. 14). Bruce suggests that
"with maturity comes a stability born of spiritual experience."[33]
This maturity of the child of God is not attained in isolation.
He cannot be "a man in Christ" and an absolute individualist.
He must recognize his relation and indebtedness to the Christian community. His maturity will be achieved, to a considerable
degree, within and through his fellowship in the community of
the redeemed. The community and the individual are closely
interrelated.

One purpose of the Christian community is the maturing of
the individual. "The aim of the Church is nothing less than to
produce men and women who have in them the reflection of
Jesus Christ Himself."[34] In turn, the community as a historical
community in contrast to a transcendental community, an idea
also prevalent in Paul's epistles, can mature and achieve its purposes in the world only through the increasing maturity of the
individuals who are members of the body. "The whole frame
grows through the due activity of each part, and builds itself
up in love" (v. 16, NEB). The growth for the whole and for
the component parts is "into him who is the head, into Christ."
Here is the real secret to the growth and maturity of the child of
God and also of the Christian community or the church of
Christ. The limb or the branch does not draw its sustenance from
other limbs or branches. It, along with them, has a direct contact

with the Head of the body. This is the secret to the vitality of the Christian's life and of the Christian church.

DOMESTIC RELATIONS

In Ephesians, as in Colossians, Paul discusses domestic relations near the close of the epistle. The following sentence serves as a transition and as a basis for what is to follow: "Be subject to one another out of reverence for Christ" (5:21). This is a general admonition. Christians are free men in Christ, but they are to surrender voluntarily their freedom for the sake of Christ and His cause. They are free from all men but are to become the slaves of all. This, which is a basic principle of our Christian faith, is applied in a special way in Ephesians five and six to domestic relations. Whatever subjection is involved, however, is to be colored, determined, and motivated by "reverence for Christ." Mackay calls this "reverence for Christ" an ethical principle and "the norm or standard of Christian social behavior."[35]

Each of the domestic relations—husbands and wives, parents and children, masters and servants—is to be maintained "in the Lord." Paul is here addressing the Christian community. He is not considering the divided home where the husband or wife is not a Christian. He touches on this matter in 1 Corinthians 7. In Ephesians he is discussing a family where the members are "in Christ." The latter is plainly true of the husband and wife and seems to be implied in the other relationships. The basic principles, however, would be the same for non-Christian as for Christian homes. The Christian ideal serves as a norm for non-Christian as well as Christian relationships.

Let us briefly notice in a more specific way what Paul said concerning the relations within the family circle. The wife is to be subject to her husband "as to the Lord." Husbands are to love their wives as Christ loved the church, and He loved the church enough to give His life for her. Children are to obey their parents "in the Lord," a phrase that is subject to varied interpretations. Fathers are to bring up their children "in the discipline and instruction of the Lord." Slaves are to be obedient to their earthly masters "as to Christ," rendering their service "as to the Lord." They are always to recognize that they are "servants of Christ, doing the will of God from the heart," remembering that they will be rewarded by their Lord. Masters should remember that they and their slaves have the same "Master . . . in heaven, and there is no partiality with him." And let us remember that all of these relationships are to be maintained "out of reverence for Christ." What a difference it would make in the home, in the community, and in human relations in general if men and women were motivated by love and reverence for Christ.

RECURRING EXHORTATIONS

There are a number of exhortations in addition to those that have already been mentioned. As one would expect, most of these are in the latter half or the hortatory section of the epistle. These emphasize again the close relation of theology and ethics.

Paul opens the applied or hortatory portion of the letter by saying, "I therefore, a prisoner for the Lord, beg ["entreat," NEB] you to lead a life worthy of the calling to which you have been called." They had been called into fellowship with Christ. They were admonished to lead a life worthy of that relationship. There are both negative and positive aspects of such a worthy life. Here Paul gives a balanced perspective with a closing emphasis on positive Christian living. He sums up the matter by saying, "Put off your old nature . . . and put on the new nature, created after the likeness of God in true righteousness and holiness" (4:22-24). He spells out, to some degree, both the negative and positive aspects of the Christian life.[36] closing with the positive statement: "Be kind to one another, tenderhearted, forgiving one another, as God in Christ forgave you" (4:32). The last phrase expresses both example and motive. It seems logical to follow that statement with the exhortation: "Therefore be imitators of God, as beloved children" (5:1). Here is the goal of the Christian life: Christians are to be like their heavenly Father.

There are three exhortations in which Paul uses the word "walk," which is a favorite expression of his.[37] He admonishes the Ephesians to "walk in love, as Christ loved us and gave himself up for us" (5:2), to "walk as children of light . . . and try to learn what is pleasing to the Lord" (5:8, 10), and to "walk . . . as wise" men (5:15), which means that they will "understand what the will of the Lord is" (5:17). If they walk as wise men they will not get drunk with wine but they will "be filled with the spirit" (5:18). To walk in love, in light, and in wisdom is to walk in the way of the Lord, to walk in obedience to and in fellowship with Him.

The closing hortatory paragraph (6:10-20) also reveals the interpenetration of theology and ethics. The Ephesians were admonished to "be strong in the Lord and in the strength of his might" (v. 10). They are to "put on the whole armor of God" (v. 11) which includes defensive and offensive implements or weapons. These are all related to the Lord; they are part of the armor of the Lord. They are to gird their "loins with truth" (v. 14), to "put on the breastplate of righteousness" (v. 14), to cover their feet "with the equipment of the gospel of peace" (v. 15). They are to take "the shield of faith," "the helmet of salvation" (v. 17), and the "sword of the Spirit, which is the word of God" (v. 17). The two closing exhortations which belong together are: "Pray at all times in the Spirit" and "Keep alert with all perseverance" (v. 18).

Carver sums up the multiple contributions of Ephesians as follows:

> The philosophy of religion finds here its ultimate principles. Christian theology has no fundamental teaching that is omitted here, and the teachings are here held in balance such as is possible only when integrated in an architectonic concept which combines all elements in a natural relationship. Christian ethics finds here their source and sanction, their aim and end, their persuasion and their power.[38]

Chapter 3

THE CHRISTIAN AND WORLD CITIZENSHIP

The Christian is a citizen of two worlds—this world and the next world; of two kingdoms—the kingdom of Caesar, and the kingdom of Christ.

As a citizen of this world, he is a citizen of his local community, county, state, nation, and the broader human community. His primary responsibility in each case should be to the broader community.

It is assumed that the Christian will participate in the life of the world. He cannot count for Christ in the world if he isolates himself from that world. But he should also remember that he will not count for Christ unless he participates in the life of the world as a Christian. The word that should precede, define, and limit every role he plays is the word "Christian." He may be an employee or an employer, but he is a *Christian* employee or employer. He may be a white man or a Negro, but he is a *Christian* white man or a *Christian* Negro. He may be a citizen of the United States or of the Soviet Union, but he is a *Christian* citizen. Every citizenship obligation and opportunity will be considered a part of his total stewardship responsibility.

Our main problem is to determine, as far as possible, how the Christian can function effectively as a citizen of the world. A complete answer to this problem would require much more space than we can give to it. All we can do is to suggest a few things in rather broad outline.

In the first portion of this paper we will suggest three things that are essential if the Christian is to be an effective citizen of the world: (1) He must be an intelligent citizen. (2) He must cultivate a sound historical perspective. (3) He must maintain a transcendent orientation or point of reference. Following a brief discussion of these three things, we shall state some assumptions and convictions, and then make a few statements concerning the relation of evangelism and ethics, and the relative emphasis on the individual and the social in our Christian faith.

AN INTELLIGENT CITIZEN

The Christian cannot be an effective citizen of the world unless he possesses a relatively high degree of general intelligence. He must also maintain a high level of political intelligence. This means, among other things, that he must be alert to social, economic, political, moral, and religious trends and issues.

No issue is more important or comprehensive than the fact that the United States, Western civilization, and the world are in the midst of a major revolution or crisis.[1] Almost every other problem or issue that plagues our nation and our world is related directly to the world crisis. For example, the evident struggle of the world for some type of political unification[2] is a phase of and a factor in the crisis. Many scholars believe that the present period of chaos, confusion, and conflict will continue until such a unification is achieved.

Closely related to the preceding is the abidingly perplexing problem of war and peace.[3] The church and the Christian conscience have struggled with this issue through the centuries. The problem has become more acute in the contemporary period when man has achieved the capacity to destroy his civilization.

At this point all we are attempting to do is to list a number of the problems or issues of the contemporary world. These are the issues, some of which will be discussed later, that a Christian must understand if he is to be an effective citizen of the world. Another issue that continues to challenge the Christian mind and conscience is the relation of the races.[4] In turn, our racial problems cannot be understood apart from the restless movement of the masses of the world. And this restless movement of the masses is an expression of and a major factor in the world crisis.

The intelligent Christian citizen needs also to understand the nature of contemporary "isms" that challenge our way of life. These "isms" or movements are also closely related to the major crisis in the West and the world. They are both evidences of and factors in the increasing seriousness of the crisis. We are thinking particularly of three closely related movements: communism, materialism, and secularism.

If the Christian is to be an effective citizen of the contemporary world, he must know what communism[5] is, what it claims to be able to do, and what it has done. He should be acquainted with its strengths and its weaknesses. He should be able to appraise objectively its criticisms of capitalism, democracy, and Christianity. The Christian, as a world citizen, should be able to make a distinction between communism as an economic program and as a philosophy or as a religion. He should know that communism has made a religion of economic determinism or of its dialectical materialism. It has its orthodox line, its prophets and its heretics, its sacred writings, its messianic hope, and its faith in world triumph. Since communism represents primarily an ideological approach to the problems of life, we should recognize that it *cannot* be defeated on the battlefield. If it is to be defeated, it must be met and defeated primarily in the realm of ideas and ideals. And, if the battle is to be won it must be more than a purely defensive battle. We should understand that there is some evidence in the contemporary period of divisions within the communist ranks. It seems apparent in some cases that national loyalty and pride are stronger than ideological purity or orthodoxy.

Another movement, if it can properly be called a movement, that is an important factor in our world is materialism. It is a threat to our whole way of life. For many of the people in our nation and in the West the material values have become the supreme values of life. To a distressing degree moral and spiritual values have been relegated to roles of secondary importance. This represents an inversion of values. This is one reason why communism cannot be the solution for the problems of the West or of the world in general. Communism makes the material supreme. Everything is explained in terms of the material.

Secularism,[6] the other of the three movements previously mentioned, is broader than materialism. It includes every area of life and not just the material. The word "secular" in contrast to "sacred" is a good word. However, when the secular divorces itself from the sacred and refuses to recognize its dependence upon and subserviency to the sacred it becomes a curse to man. Rightly or wrongly, this is what we mean by secularism.

Secularism does not necessarily mean a denial of the existence of God or of the sacred realm. It merely means an ignoring of God or of the sacred realm. It is living as if God did not exist. The final point of reference for all of life is in the here-and-now and not in the hereafter. Man and his society is the final authority and not God. It is possible that the main threat to the United States and to Western civilization comes from materialism and secularism rather than from communism. The threat is more insidious, and hence it is more dangerous. We are less prepared to meet it. Really, the threat from communism will be a real threat only when materialism and secularism, like termites, have undermined the foundations of our way of life.

A HISTORICAL PERSPECTIVE

If a Christian is to live effectively as a world citizen he must not only be an intelligent citizen, he must also cultivate a sound historical perspective.

In a very real sense we can never understand anything fully

unless we understand it historically. This is true of the world issues that have been mentioned. We cannot know how to face these issues and how to make a constructive contribution to their resolution unless we understand something of their roots in the past. We cannot sense the direction in which the world is now moving unless we have some insight into the route it has traveled.

The limitations of space will not permit even a sketch of the historical background for every world problem or issue. Let us use, for purposes of illustration, two issues. First, let us consider in outline form the relation of the church and the state.[7]

There have been four major periods or epochs during the Christian era in regard to the relation of the church and the state. It should be understood that these periods cannot be separated by a hard and fast line. They overlap considerably.

1. During the first three centuries the church was a minority group under an indifferent or hostile state.

2. From Constantine to the Reformation, the church and the state, at least in theory, were partners; a partnership in which the church claimed and in the main succeeded in establishing its dominant role.

3. During the period from the Reformation to the Enlightenment, there was a unity of the church and the state, but due to the rise of the national states and the consequent division of Christendom, the unity took the form of parallel establishments.

4. From the days of the Enlightenment until today the point of departure has not been the nation, or the church, but the individual. The doctrine of the separation of the church and the state arose and became effective during this period. However, it was present to some degree among the sectarians all the time.

Rather consistently there have been three major theories concerning the relation of the church and the state. Each one of these is also contemporary to a degree.

1. Theory of identification. To be a citizen of the state is to be a member of the church. This is the general position where there is an established church.

2. Theory of domination. This may be domination of the state by the church or of the church by the state.

3. Theory of separation. This may be an unfriendly separation such as exists in the Soviet Union, or a friendly separation such as we have in the United States.

For a second illustration of the value of historical perspective let us consider the relation of the secular and the sacred. An insight into the historical developments concerning the relation of the secular and the sacred will give one a better insight into the contemporary crisis and into many of the factors contributing to that crisis.

The relation throughout Christian history of these two broad areas rather closely parallels the relation of church and state, and the relation of the church to the world in general.

Possibly before we consider the relation of the secular and the sacred the terms should be distinguished. By "sacred" is meant those things that are concerned primarily with eternal or spiritual values. "Secular" refers to temporal things in contrast to the sacred or the eternal. Now, let us sketch the relation of the two.

1. In the early centuries of the Christian era the two were divorced. The secular area was considered unholy by most Christians. They believed that the Christian should have just as little to do with the world and the things of the world as absolutely necessary. This included the amusements of the world, business activities, political affairs, and war. On the other hand, and almost inevitably, the secular maintained its independence of the sacred.

2. There developed a struggle between the church and the world, between the secular and the sacred.

3. The sacred, in the main, won the battle and dominated the secular, forcing it into subserviency. The secular lost practically all of its autonomy.

4. The secular asserted its independence. This was a part of the fragmentation of the old unified civilization which took place at the time of the Renaissance and the Reformation.

5. For some time the secular areas such as economic life and politics retained a sense of relatedness to and dependence upon the sacred. The point of reference, or the basis of judgment, even within these areas was still considered to be outside the secular area.

6. Gradually, the secular asserted its independence of the sacred. It became a law unto itself. It lost the sense of the eternal. This was and is seen in such expressions as "business for business' sake," "art for art's sake," "science for science's sake." These and other secular areas not only became independent of religion but also of God. They tended to recognize no eternal values or laws. They had their own laws. They made their own rules.

7. The sacred, where retained, was pushed to a small segment of man's life. It became one of many compartments. Too frequently the church itself accepted this compartmental status or idea.

8. The secular tended increasingly to become sacred itself. It tended to claim to contain within itself the supreme values of life. It became a competitor with the truly sacred. Demanding the supreme loyalty of its followers, it became a false religion with false gods.

9. The ultimate results of such a procedure are or will be self-defeating. The secular alone cannot satisfy the deeper hungers of men. A self-sufficient secularism will ultimately destroy itself. The sacred and particularly the eternal God, who gives meaning and coherence to the secular and the sacred, cannot indefinitely be pushed to one side. We are beginning to see that the secular must retain a point of reference outside of itself or it ultimately will destroy itself and the civilization it builds. The Eternal must have a voice in things or there will be a collapse.

The preceding, in broad outline, traces one approach to a study of the contemporary world crisis.

A TRANSCENDENT ORIENTATION

To be most effective the Christian citizen must not only be intelligent and cultivate a historical perspective, he must also maintain a transcendent orientation or point of reference. What does this mean and what will it do for him? If one has an abidingly transcendent point of reference:

1. He will believe that his God is active in the world and that He is on the side of the right, the good, the true.

2. He will attempt to sense the direction in which God is moving in our world and will seek to catch step with Him.

3. He will believe that all areas of his life and all phases of the life of his nation and the world must ultimately recognize their dependence on God and dedicate themselves to the service of God and mankind.

4. He will have an abiding faith in a sovereign God whose overall purpose will be triumphant in the world; he will believe that God will have the last word.

5. He will recognize that above the kingdom of this world is the kingdom or rule of God.

6. He will recognize that his supreme and final obedience belongs to God and not to the state or to the church.

7. He will seek to retain a constant sense of the eternal; he will make the eternal values supreme in his life.

If the Christian citizen can achieve and maintain such a transcendent, eternal orientation in his life, it will give to him a sense of purpose and patience, poise and perseverance as he follows what he considers to be the divine purpose of his life and the will of God for his world. Underneath the tensions of his life, which are the common lot of those who take seriously the demands of Christ, will be a peace that passeth understanding, a peace that comes only to those who are conscious of the presence of the Sovereign God who is our loving heavenly Father.

ASSUMPTIONS AND CONVICTIONS

It has been suggested that the effective Christian citizen must be intelligent, must cultivate a historical perspective, and must maintain a transcendent orientation or point of reference. It may sound like moving backward, but he must also make certain assumptions and have certain convictions concerning the Christian life. These will help to explain his continuing concern for the world and the peoples of the world. They will give him the inner drive or urge to go out into the world to live his faith. They will give him the courage to go on regardless of the resistance that he faces.

A basic assumption that needs to be restated over and over again is that the Christian religion is as broad as life itself. It is concerned with the totality of life. It could not be otherwise when the God we worship is the sovereign God of the universe, the God of the street as well as of the sanctuary. The Christ, who fully revealed the Father and who is our Lord and Saviour, is supposed to become a living reality not only in our individual lives but also in the structures of society and in the entire fabric of our social order. By means of redeemed individuals, who are in the world to reveal Christ, He is to live in and find expression through the family, the work or play group, the community, the state, the nation, the world.

This means that we believe and seek to promote the idea that the spirit and the principles of Jesus are to be applied to every area of our lives. We are to reveal Him in the church but also in the home; He is to live in us and have freedom to express Himself through us in the shop or in the store, on the street or on the highway, as well as in the sanctuary. He is to be permitted to live in us and express Himself through us on Monday as well as on Sunday. We believe that the obligations of the Christian life rest as squarely on the Christian lawyer, the doctor, the merchant, the farmer, or the housewife as they do upon the pastor, the denominational worker, or the missionary.

We further believe that the outstanding weakness of historic and contemporary Christianity has been and is the ethical or moral weakness. Southern Baptists, for example, have many wonderfully strong qualities. On the other hand, we have failed, to a distressing degree, to face up to the moral requirements of our Christian faith. This is so noticeably true that we are in real danger of becoming many *but not much.*

This weakness has been especially noticeable in regard to the broader moral and social problems of the world in general and of the Southern region in particular. It is a rather serious reflection on us that we have not done more to alleviate or to solve some of the pressing problems of the area where we are the largest religious body, and even in some sections larger in numbers than all other denominations combined. The area where we are strongest is plagued with some of the most acute and perplexing problems found in any section of the United States or in the world. Frequently we have been so conservative and hesitant about applying Christ's spirit and teachings to real life situations that we have actually aided and abetted the defenders of old patterns of life—patterns that are definitely sub-Christian if not actually anti-Christian. These patterns in many cases are being challenged and are doomed to die.

It appears that many of us have been so muddled in our thinking that we believe that our theological conservatism forces us to be conservative in all other areas of our lives. What is needed desperately in our world is an effective working synthesis of a basically conservative theology and a social liberalism.

EVANGELISM AND ETHICS

We have been persistent in winning the unsaved to Christ. All of us hope that we shall never lose our historic evangelistic fervor, that we shall continue to have a warm, searching heart for the lost, and a sense of urgency about seeking men for Christ.

It is unfortunate, however, that some who are fervent in winning the unsaved tend to belittle and even to ridicule the moral or ethical approach to the problems of life. It is suggested that all one has to do is to lead the individual to accept Christ. The implication is that this experience will automatically solve all his problems and will guarantee right attitudes toward all the issues of life.

Slogans are perfected such as "Christ is the answer." We agree that He is the answer, but what is meant by the slogan? How is He to be the answer? How is the answer to be implemented? Are redeemed men supposed to help Christ to be the answer? Is the answer for all of life's problems to be found in the initial decision when the individual accepts Christ? Or, does the complete answer include the things Jesus taught and the example He set? How is Christ the answer for the problems that so persistently plague our nation and our world?

Those who would largely divorce evangelism from ethics, who would fail to give much place to moral instruction in the development of Christian character, and who, in many cases, would resist the application of the Christian message to social relations and issues, fail to remember at least three things.

First, they fail to remember the one who has been won to Christ is a babe in Christ. As a babe he does not know innately what is right or wrong for him to do. Neither does he inevitably have the inner discipline or dynamic to do what he knows is right.

Second, such a one also fails to remember that Christ is not only Saviour but that he is also Lord. Just a casual check of a good concordance will reveal that Christ is called Lord many times more frequently than he is referred to as Saviour. The original decision that makes one a child of God involves vastly more than a rather passive acceptance of the salvation that is offered him in Christ. It involves the acceptance of Christ, who brings the salvation. He is a living person. He comes into the life of the child of God. He lives in him and expresses Himself through him. It is a vital, life-changing union. He is the vine, we are the branches. We become new creations in Christ Jesus. He is in us and we in Him. He is the Lord of our lives. We have committed ourselves and all that we are and have to Him.

A third thing frequently forgotten is that while original Christianity was anxious that individuals should be brought to Christ, it was also concerned that those individuals should live a consistent life for Christ. It was Jesus Himself who said, "Go . . . and make disciples," but who also said, "teaching them to observe [to obey] all that I have commanded you" (Matt. 28:18-20).

The emphasis that faith without works is dead is not only the message of James but of Jesus, of Paul, of John, and of the prophets before them. Jesus stated it thus: "You will know them by their fruits." It is he who raises the searching question, "Are grapes gathered from thorns, or figs from thistles?" (Matt. 7:16). The obvious answer is "No." The sound tree bears good fruit, but the bad tree bears evil fruit. Plain-spoken John says, "By this it may be seen who are the children of God, and who are the children of the devil: whoever does not do right is not of God, nor he who does not love his brother" (1 John 3:10). If I read my New Testament correctly it does not say, "If you are a child of God you *should* do so and so," but rather, "If you are a child of God you *will* do so and so."

INDIVIDUAL AND SOCIAL

There are some who will argue as follows: "Much of what you have said I will accept. However, I believe Christianity originally was centered exclusively in the individual and that contemporary Christianity should limit its concern to individuals. There is no place in the Christian religion for a social ethic."

Let us assume, for the sake of argument, that Christianity is and should be primarily if not exclusively interested in the individual. When this is assumed there are still some important questions to ask and to answer. A basic one is: "What phase of the life of the individual should Christianity be concerned about?" Some additional questions that might be asked are: "Should Christianity and Christian leaders limit their concern to the individual's eternal well-being?" "Should the interest be limited to saving him from hell and for heaven?" "Or, should the Christian forces seek to lead the saved individual into deepening fellowship and cooperation with God?"

If the last is a part of our purpose, what is our conception of God? Do we think of Him as a more or less uninterested spectator, living in high aloofness from the affairs of the world? Or, do we think of Him as vitally interested and active in the affairs of the world? If God is active in the world, does He expect His children to cooperate with Him in doing His work in the world? One's answers to these and similar questions will make a great deal of difference in his viewpoint concerning the Christian life.

The preceding questions have not been asked to ridicule the otherworldly emphasis which is still very prevalent in one form or another. It should be admitted, as stressed previously, that no Christian will live most effectively for God unless he retains an eternal point of reference in his life. He can correctly think of himself as a stranger here within a foreign land. But he is *here*. He lives in two worlds and cannot escape his responsibilities to either. He is an ambassador *of* the Eternal but also an ambassador *to* the temporal, to the here-and-now.

As the representative of the King, the Christian is to pray for the coming of the Kingdom or the reign of God among men. He is not only to pray for that Kingdom, but he is also to seek it. He prays and he works with the conviction that the Kingdom comes as God's will is done on earth as it is in heaven. It comes as God's righteousness and justice find fuller expression in him, among men in general, and in the world.

The Christian's relation and twofold obligation to God and to man are clearly revealed in the reply Jesus gave to the lawyer who asked him, "Teacher, which is the great command in the law?" Jesus replied that the great and first commandment was that one should love God supremely, that this love should include the total personality. Then He added, "And a second is like it, You shall love your neighbor as yourself." The second is like the first; it is a commandment of love. But the second is like the first also in importance. They belong together. One cannot fulfill the basic moral and religious requirements of God without both. If one loved God supremely he would keep the first table of the law. If he loved his neighbor as himself he would keep the second table. And these two tables summarize the demands of the basic moral law of the Old Testament. No wonder it is said, after Jesus gave these two great commandments, "On these two commandments depend all the law and the prophets" (see Matt. 22:36-40).

The question still remains: "Who is my neighbor?" This question asked by the lawyer, according to Luke's record, was answered, if answered at all, indirectly rather than directly by Jesus. He told the lawyer the story of the Good Samaritan. There may be some doubt whether or not Jesus really answered the lawyer's question. Certainly He refused to build any fences for him. At the close of the story Jesus asked the lawyer a searching question, and one far more significant than the lawyer's question. The question by Jesus was, "Which of these three, do you think, proved neighbor to the man who fell among the robbers?" (see Luke 10:25-37). It is far more important to know *how* one can be a neighbor than *who* one's neighbor is.

If living the Christian life involves right relations with God and with one's fellowman, what are the areas where the latter is to find expression? Certainly it includes right relations with all individuals with whom one has contact.

The individual may be a brother, a husband, a son, a father, a neighbor, an employee, an employer, a white man, a black man, a citizen of the United States, or a citizen of the world. In other words, even if we begin with the individual, there is no place to stop until we reach the furtherest limits of our world. If one is a follower of Christ, to repeat a former statement, he must place a defining and significantly limiting word in front of each of the above. He is not just a son or a father, he is a *Christian* son or a *Christian* father. So in all the other relations of his life, the word "Christian" is to precede and to be underscored in front of every role he plays in life.

As Christ's representative, or, possibly better, as Christ incarnate, he is to let Christ live in him and express Himself through him. This will mean that all he does for Christ and for his fellowman will be done naturally because of the inner drive and motivation that comes from the indwelling Christ. This means, among other things, that his life will be an embodiment of *agape*, or the divine type of love. This *agape* type of love gives itself unselfishly to the one loved. It will love even the unlovely and the unworthy.

Letting Christ live in us and through us also will mean that we shall come to understand something of the meaning and the significance of the cross. We shall come to see that the ethic of Jesus was basically an ethic of the cross. It is the cross as a symbol of self-denial and self-sacrifice that gives unity to His ethical teachings. If we are to go with Him we must take up our cross daily or day by day and keep on following Him.

This, however, does not exhaust the Christian's responsibilities. He is also to do what he can to make every group to which he belongs conform, as far as possible, to the spirit and to the teachings of Jesus.

Surely when we see how inclusive the living of the Christian life really is, we are convinced that even the most mature of us have not begun to comprehend the richness in Christ and the demands He makes upon our lives. When the depth and breadth of the Christian life is understood, it is seen also that the term "Christian" is relative. If we measure our lives in terms of daily living, the best among us are very imperfectly Christian. One comes to understand that being fully Christian involves not only justification, a once for all experience, but it also involves sanctification, which is a process. There is a very real sense in which we have been saved (justification), are in the process of being saved (sanctification), and ultimately will be saved (glorification).

The test of our lives is the direction in which we are moving. Are we more fully Christian today than yesterday, this week than last week, this month than last month, this year than last year? Are we working more effectively today than in the past to apply Christ's spirit and principles to every area of our lives and to every phase of the life of our world? Or, possibly a better way to express the same idea is to ask, "Are we letting Christ possess us and express Himself through us more fully with each passing day?" May every one of us at the end of our earthly journey hear the Master's "Well done, thou good and faithful servant."

Chapter 4

THE CHURCH AND WORLD PROBLEMS

The basis for Christian concern for the world and the peoples of the world is not only grounded in the biblical revelation; it also naturally evolves from the nature of the church and the resultant relation of the church to the world. There is a sense in which the church is set against the world, but there is also a very real sense in which the church is set in the world as God's representative to the world. This dual relation of the church to the world and hence to the problems of the world results from and is expressive of the twofold nature of the church.

DIVINE-HUMAN NATURE OF THE CHURCH

The Corinthian letters were addressed by Paul to "the church of God which is at Corinth." This suggests something of major significance concerning the church. The church is the church of God. Its divine nature means that it can never be perfectly at home in any human society. As Stephen Neill says, it is "pledged in perpetuity to a pilgrim condition."[1] There is a sense in which "it is not created by its members but only organized by them. . . . Its essential purpose is not decided by its members; it is only interpreted by them."[2] One of its chief purposes is to make men and the society of men conscious of the presence of and their responsibility to the living God. The spire of its building points symbolically upward toward God. Its members are so to live as to point men to the "Lamb of God, who takes away the sin of the world."

The church, however, is not only divine; it is, in its organizational embodiment, also a human society or institution—it is at "Corinth." It is *A Treasure in Earthen Vessels*.[3] As a divine institution or organism, it stands outside of history and speaks to history; as a human institution it is immersed in history. It cannot escape, but it should not be dominated by its humanity. It ministers to human beings in a particular geographic area with distinctive problems and perspectives, but it should never forget that it ministers in the name of God. Let us repeat, however, that it is the church of God at Atlanta, Birmingham, Chicago, Los Angeles, Dallas, or New York, and its location does make some difference.

The divine-human nature of the church creates some problems for it. The more it lets its divine nature express itself, the more it discovers that what it preaches, teaches, and practices is in conflict with the world. This creates tension between the church and the world, but this tension is not exclusively a problem. Without it the church cannot lift the world toward God's ideal for the world. Possibly it should be suggested that the tension may become so great between the church and the world that the church will be unable any longer to minister effectively to the world. Comparatively few churches, however, need this warning. It possibly should be added that a church as well as an individual Christian might occasionally serve the cause of Christ best by taking dead seriously the divine demands and living dangerously for the Lord even if it means martyrdom. At least we would discover anew the meaning of the cross.

When both the divine and human natures or aspects of the church are kept in proper balance, there is created an almost inevitable tension within the church itself. It is a tension or conflict between its basic nature or inner genius and its outer expression as a human institution. There is frequent conflict within the fellowship of the church between the more mature and the less mature, between the prophetic voices in the pulpit and the pew and the organizational men, the status seekers, and the stand-patters in both pulpit and pew. This tension within the church may create some serious problems for the church, but it is also largely the source and secret to whatever creative drive the church retains.

THE CHURCH'S STRATEGIES

Much of the preceding has been rather idealistic. Many, and possibly most, churches do not maintain a balance between their divine and their human natures. They frequently adopt attitudes and strategies regarding the world and the problems of the world that would not be acceptable from the preceding perspective. They may overmagnify the divine nature of the church and practice the withdrawal or the rejection strategy. And, incidentally, this strategy is not restricted to a few minor sects. Any church is practicing to some degree the withdrawal strategy when it restricts Christian activities to the church building and to the Lord's day. It tends, so far as the world is concerned, to become a fellowship of the indifferent rather than a fellowship of the concerned.

On the other hand, churches may largely lose the sense of their divine nature and follow the identification strategy. They tend to identify the church with the world and to become a defender of the particular community and culture in which they find themselves. These two strategies—withdrawal and identification—are comparable to what H. Richard Niebuhr labels "Christ Against Culture" and "The Christ of Culture."[4]

The first of these strategies—withdrawal from the world—tends to be prevalent when the church is surrounded by an unfriendly persecuting world, or when the Christian body is a minority group. In contrast, it seems more or less natural for the church to accommodate itself to the world, if not actually to identify itself with the world, when it is in a relatively friendly world and particularly when it becomes strong in numbers and finances and has attained considerable prestige in the world. Such a church tends to use worldly standards as its measure of success, to perpetuate the class divisions of the community in which it finds itself, and to become little less secularized than the world itself. It frequently identifies itself with an order of society that is already passing away. This is particularly unfortunate when the church is in a revolutionary age such as the contemporary period.

We are suffering today from too close an identification of the church with the world. This is particularly true of the larger, better established churches and denominations. As a result, we are afflicted with a mild sort of religiosity; we are threatened with the menace of mediocrity. As Dr. Elton Trueblood says, "We are equally shocked at hearing the faith denied or seeing it practiced." To use an expression of Norman Pittenger, religion for many church members has become a peripheral or an adjectival matter. It is no longer the center of life. It is not the total to which everything else is subservient. As a result, there is a disturbing discrepancy between the numerical size of many churches and denominations and their influence.

The church in the contemporary world, in the main, counts itself among the privileged. It has thrived in the present world order and it is inclined to defend that order. This usually means that the church defends the privileged rather than the underprivileged. This, in turn, reverses the historic emphasis of the prophetic element of our faith. The prophetic note is largely lacking. If a prophet happens to arise in the pulpit or the pew, an effort is usually made to silence him or to relegate him to a place where he will disturb the status quo just as little as absolutely necessary. One of the greatest sins, from the perspective of such a church, or denomination, is to challenge or to disturb the present order.

There is something, however, in the very nature of the church that cries out against such an identification of the church with the culture in which it finds itself. The church cannot escape entirely the judgment of its divine nature and of the message it proclaims. Herein is its main hope. Over and over again it is renewed from within through the presence of the resurrected Lord in the message it preaches and teaches but fails to practice.

The words of the Great Commission continually ring in the ears of the church: All authority has been given to me—not only in heaven but also on earth. Since this is true you are to go and make disciples or learners and through baptism you are to lead them to identify themselves with me and my movement. But you are not to stop there. Your task is not complete until you have taught them to observe or to obey *all* that I have commanded you. *All* of the children of God are to go to *all* the world with *all* of the Gospel. There can be no limits. The beginning place is with the individual, but every aspect of the life of that individual is to be brought under the lordship of Christ. In turn, in fellowship with other like-minded persons, he is to seek to bring every aspect of our common life under the righteous rule or reign of God. He will recognize that the kingdom is God's and that it is a gift from God, but paradoxically what God gives must also be fought for and won.

THE INDIVIDUAL AND THE WORLD

The church is concerned primarily with individuals. Its concern, however, is not restricted to any one segment of their lives. For example, the church recognizes that a basic purpose of its total program is to bring men and women face to face with Christ and to witness to them concerning His power to save. However, this evangelistic function is much broader than many have thought. The faith that saves is "a righteous and a dynamic faith." The great faith chapter (Hebrews 11) illustrates this fact. Faith led the great heroes and heroines of God to *do* something. Theirs was a faith that led to action.

Furthermore, the recognition of the lordship of Christ is just as essential in the initial Christian experience as the acceptance of Christ as Saviour. One cannot accept Him as Saviour without receiving Him as Lord. And if He is Lord, where does His lordship stop? We believe that there can be no limits. This means, among other things, that the church is concerned for the totality of the life of the individual. Just as no limit can be set for the lordship of Christ in the life of the individual child of God, neither can such a limit be set for the congregation of God's redeemed ones anywhere in the world.

Because of its deep concern for individuals, the church is also concerned about what community and world conditions do for and to those individuals—individuals who have been created in the image of God, and for whom Christ died. This helps to explain the church's concern about slums, juvenile delinquency, salacious literature, beverage alcohol, gambling, corruption in big business and big labor, dishonesty in high places, class and color prejudice, and many other evils in our world.

The church may be deeply interested in persons, but its concern for them and their well-being is not on a solid basis unless it stems from a "thus saith the Lord." A study of the messages of God's great prophets will reveal that their emphasis on righteousness and justice stemmed primarily from their concern for the will of God rather than for the welfare of man. They certainly were concerned about people, particularly the underprivileged, but that concern resulted from the fact that they saw men through the eyes of God. It may be that some of us, and many of our churches, lack in passion and concern for people because we have failed to hear the voice of God as He spoke through the prophets and particularly through His Son. We recognize God as the creator of the world, but too many of us tend to consider Him an absentee landlord. Many of us have not seen as clearly as we should have that He cannot be the sovereign God of the universe unless He is sovereign over all. This means that He is concerned with and is an active participant in all of life. He does not sit at the side of the stream of life and watch the world go by. He is not a disinterested or even an interested spectator. No, He is the most dynamic and creative force within history.

Let us sum up what we have said so far by suggesting that every aspect of the life of the individual and society is of concern to God and hence should be of concern to the church which is supposed to be committed to seek, to interpret, and to do God's will.

WORLD IN CRISIS

Once the church becomes concerned for the world, it finds that the issues and problems are baffling. This is true not only because of the number of the problems but also because of their complexity. The church runs considerable risk if it takes a stand on any issue. There is always some possibility that its stand will be wrong. This does not mean, however, that the church should fold its hands and have nothing to do with the problems of the world. It is far better to run the risk of making some mistakes than to do nothing.

The biggest, most complex, and most comprehensive of those problems is the world crisis. Ours is a revolutionary world. There are so many crises that one crisis has not been eased before another arises. There are crises in the Orient, in Africa, in the Middle East, in America, in Europe, and everywhere. Most nations are aware of crises within their national life—sectional and cultural.

There is something deeper and more meaningful, however, than these localized crises. Our world is in the midst of the most serious crisis that it has known since the days of the Renaissance and the Reformation. If this is correct, then it seems relatively sure that out of the contemporary crisis will come a new way of life—economically, politically, and even possibly religiously.

While this crisis or revolution is worldwide in scope, there is a sense in which it is centered in Western civilization. At least the crises in other parts of the world are related to and stem, to a degree, from the crisis in Western civilization.

The crisis within the West can be described in a number of ways. Civilizations are built or unified around an integrating center. That center contains the basic concepts, or the ends in contrast to the means or techniques of that civilization. In a very real sense, the integrating center of a civilization is its religion. Civilizations are usually threatened either because of the infiltration of the basic concepts or values of a competing civilization or because of internal decay which accompanies and is a factor in the disintegration of the integrating center of the civilization. The latter is usually the major factor in the decay and threatened collapse of a more advanced civilization. Its integrating center no longer retains the capacity to serve as a sort of magnet to attract and hold in proper relation all of the various aspects of that civilization.

Another way of expressing the same thing is to say that a civilization declines and is threatened with collapse when it loses its faith. This is the chief threat to Western civilization in the contemporary period. We do not have the time or space to trace the route our civilization has travelled. There are two main sources for the cluster of ideas that formed its integrating center. Those sources were humanism, representing its Renaissance strain, and the Christian movement, particularly Protestantism, representing the Reformation strain of its way of life. Humanism became more and more anthropocentric—exalting man apart from God. It even infiltrated Christian theology to a considerable degree. As a result of all of this, the Western world for some time before World War I had a strong but unrealistic faith in man, in science, and in the inevitable progress of history. It was believed that all man needed to solve his problems and the problems of his world was a little more knowledge, and education would give him that; a little more power, and science would give him that; and a little more freedom, and the democratic movement would provide that.

What has happened to this humanistic liberal faith? It was rudely shocked, if not actually destroyed, by World War I, the Great Depression, World War II, and now the threat of total destruction. Western man has, to a distressing degree, lost his faith not only in himself but also in his way of life. To use Trueblood's well-known expression, ours is largely "a cut-flower civilization." Through a loss of faith in its basic concepts our civilization has been cut loose from the sources of its strength and vitality. To use the title of a chapter in one of Emile Caillett's books, ours is "A Lost Radiance."

MOVEMENT OF THE MASSES

At the very time when the West was so largely losing its faith, there was a revival of hope, if not of faith, in much of the rest of the world, particularly in the Orient and in Africa. The great masses of the world began to stir. They became restless. Frank Laubach, who knows those masses as well as any American, says that their movement is inevitable and irresistible. They are seeking for freedom, for dignity and respect, for a purpose for which to live, and for a greater share in the good things of life. They no longer will be satisfied to be a subject or colonial people. A leading churchman from South India a few years ago said that "never before have so many millions of people taken part in such a rapid and radical social upheaval. In the last ten years, nearly 700 millions have gained their independence." Since then there have been additional millions who have won their independence. One evidence of the preceding is the large number of African nations admitted to the United Nations in recent years. The Asian-African block can now serve as a rather effective balance of power in the General Assembly.

What has been the source for this restless movement of the masses? One source is Western civilization itself. The more highly industrialized nations of the West have gone around the world searching for raw materials and for markets for their manufactured products. Inevitably, some of the ideas and ideals of the West went along. For example, we could not export our techniques without exporting some of our basic concepts. After a while these concepts or ideals took root, and when the people began to understand them and to take them seriously, they became restless.

The Christian movement has also been a factor in this unrest among the masses of the world. Some of the basic concepts of the West are the contributions of Christianity to the West. No one of these is more central and more significant than the worth and dignity of the individual person. The Christian missionary has also contributed, in varying degrees, to the growing unrest among the masses. The message that he has proclaimed has said that all men are created in the image of God, that Christ died for all, and that God is no respecter of persons. If men take seriously these and related ideas, they will not be satisfied with a permanently secondary status for themselves and particularly for their fellow men.

At the time when the West had so largely lost its radiance and there was a growing appropriation of the Western way by the under developed masses of the world, there arose a movement with what Caillett calls a "false radiance," but with a radiance. As Arnold Toynbee and others have suggested, that movement was a Western heresy. It was born in the West, was rejected in the West, and was adopted and adapted by the Russians and turned on the West. This movement has become the chief challenger not only of our so-called Western way of life, but also of the Christian movement.

CONCLUSION

In addition to the world crisis or revolution there are a number of other issues or problems more or less closely related to the world revolution. Among these are the relation of church and state, the challenge of communism, the struggle between management and labor along with related problems in the economic area, war and peace—a continuing and perplexing problem, the civil rights movement which cannot be understood apart from the restless movement of the masses of the world, and the so-called sex revolution with its threat to the American home and to our nation. Some of these problems will be discussed, at least to a limited degree, in the remaining chapters of this book.

This, in broad outline, is my conception of the kind of world in which we live. The battle is on for the minds, souls, and loyalties of men. That battle is being fought, to some degree, within our own country, but primarily among the marching masses of the world. It seems that whoever wins the loyalty of and provides the leadership for those masses will control the future.

Charles Malik, a Christian statesman from Lebanon and former chairman of the General Assembly of the United Nations, in his opening remarks at a Christian conference for men said: "There are three unpardonable sins today: to be flippant or superficial in the analysis of the world situation; to live and act as though halfhearted measures would avail; and to lack the moral courage to rise to the historic occasion."[5] These may be the sins of the church as well as sins of the individual child of God. For example, the church may lack the moral courage to sound the prophetic note that is so desperately needed in the contemporary period. Herbert Butterfield, a famous English historian with a challenging Christian perspective, says, "The revolutionary character of the present world situation does not call for the kind of Christianity which, in a settled world, associates itself with the defense of the existing order. It calls for the other kind of Christianity, the insurgent type, which goes back to first principles and measures the present order of things against these."[6] These first principles contain the message that our world desperately needs.

John Foster Dulles once said that "the qualities that Christ taught" are the qualities that men need "in order to deal realistically with practical problems."[7] He also said that after thirty years of dealing with international affairs he had come to the conclusion that the church's influence could be decisive in influencing the pattern of the future.[8] It should be noted that he said, "could be decisive." We must ask ourselves, however, if the contemporary church has the answers for the problems of our world and its people. We must admit that the kind of Christianity found in most of our churches today will not meet the needs of a world in crisis. The church itself is in a crisis and in need of renewal.

Part II

FAMILY PROBLEMS

The family is the most basic of all social institutions. There is a sense in which every other institution of society has evolved from the home. It is the most important of all institutions. It is a more important educational institution than the school: parents are the chief educators of their children. The home is also a more important institution for law and order than the state: the homes of a community will determine far more than any governmental agency whether or not we will have citizens who obey the laws and respect those who enforce them. The home is even a more basically important religious institution than the church. As goes the home, so goes everything else, including civilization itself.

Chapter 5

BIBLICAL FOUNDATIONS FOR FAMILY LIVING

When the Pharisees tested Jesus by asking, "Is it lawful for a man to divorce his wife on any and every ground?" (Matt. 19:3, NEB), Jesus, in his reply, went back of the law (Deut. 24:1) and its interpretation to the Lawgiver and His creative purpose. He asked them, "Have you never read that the Creator made them from the beginning male and female?" He then added, "For this reason a man shall leave his father and mother, and be made one with his wife; the two shall become one flesh. It follows that they are no longer two individuals: they are one flesh. What God hath joined together, man must not separate" (Matt. 19:4-6, NEB). This conversation of Jesus with the Pharisees is a good place to begin a search for biblical foundations for responsible family living.

THE IMAGE OF GOD

The words "from the beginning" in the statement of Jesus remind us of the opening words of the first book of the Bible: "In the beginning God." Here is summed up the biblical perspective concerning life in general. God is the source of all life. This viewpoint is found in the New Testament as well as in the Old Testament. The main difference is that the New Testament reveals Christ as an active participant in the creative work of God (John 1:3; cf. 1 Cor. 8:6, Col. 1:15-16, Heb. 1:2).

The crowning act of God's creative work was the creation of man in His own image. The fact that man was created in the image of God has considerable significance for any discussion of the family. There may be and are several interpretations of the meaning of the term "image," but any adequate explanation would include the capacity and even the necessity for communication. God is a person, man is created a person—there is no person without other persons. In a very true sense man is not only an individual but also a community. He carries within his nature the potential of the latter and demands it if he is to rise above the animal level to true personality.

Man has the capacity and really the necessity for an I-Thou relation with God and also with man. He finds his highest fulfillment in fellowship with God, but his nature also demands communication with his fellowman. The highest expression of the latter is in the husband-wife relationship. It is interesting from our viewpoint to note that two of the three Old Testament references to the image of God in man are not to man alone as an individual but to male and female (Gen. 1:26-27; 5:1-3; the other reference is Gen. 9:5-6).

It is no wonder that God said, "It is not good that the man should be alone; I will make him a helper fit for him" ["a helper to suit him," Moffatt] (Gen. 2:18). Why is it not good or advantageous for man to be alone? Some have suggested that it is not good physically for man or woman to dwell alone. A married man or woman lives longer on the average than the unmarried, and it does not just *seem* longer. This may be true, but it does not get to the depth of this expression. It is not good or advantageous for man to be alone because he was created in the image of God. This means, in the final analysis, that marriage and the home is not just grounded in the will of God but ultimately in the nature of God.

Notice that it says, "I will make him a helper fit for him," or "suited to him." Nothing could be found among God's created beings to serve as man's companion. There is a kinship between man and the animals, but there is no basis there for true companionship. Man's helpmate must be on the same level with him, must be capable of an I-Thou relation with him. This is the background for the creation of woman. When she was brought to man, he said, "This at last is bone of my bone and flesh of my flesh; she shall be called Woman, because she was taken out of Man" (Gen. 2:23).

In woman, man sees his other self. To use the marginal reading of the American Standard Version, she was one answering to him, one who complemented him, one in whom he could find his fulfillment. Men and women are made for one another like a violin and bow are made for one another; made to find their fulfillment in one another.

This implies that man and woman are created by God to fulfill distinctive functions. If the implication is correct, then we can be sure that any shifting or reversing of God's purposes will bring unfortunate results to the home and to society.

Possibly a parenthetical word should be said about what happened to the image of God in man when he sinned. That image was marred but not completely destroyed. Man became totally depraved only in the sense that every phase of his personality was affected by sin. This means, among other things, that the sexual aspects of life have felt and do feel the effects of sin.

MALE AND FEMALE

Genesis 1 reveals a close relation of the image of God concept to the creation of male and female. This means, among other things, that woman as well as man was created in the image of God, was created for fellowship with Him, and with fellow human beings. This also means that she, as well as man, is of the natural order but also has the capacity to surmount that order. As a result of this, men and women are to respect one another, are never to use one another as a mere means to an end.

The fact that God created male and female means that he has written the home into the nature of men and women. They are made for marriage.

There may be and is a place for celibacy or virginity, but it should not be exalted above marriage as has been done at times by some branches of Christendom. Marriage is the normal life for God's children. It and celibacy are both honorable, and both marriage and a religiously motivated celibacy should be entered voluntarily. It is possible that some, for various reasons, should live the celibate life. Paul, at least when he wrote 1 Corinthians 7, considered it advantageous for himself and possibly for others; but Paul, the practical moralist, steered the middle course—he commended celibacy without condemning marriage. He implied that one who should live the celibate life would have a special divine gift to do so (1 Cor. 7:7; cf. Matt. 19:12).

CREATION GOOD

Another idea in the creation story that is quite significant for our purpose is the fact that "God saw everything that he had made, and behold, it was good" (Gen. 1:31). This included male and female. It represented the Hebraic perspective concerning God's creative work. God was the creator of all; God was good; therefore, what He created was good. In contrast to much Grecian thought, the Jews considered the material or the physical as good, and hence the body and sex were good and not evil within themselves.

Even in 1 Corinthians 7, Paul, revealing a wholesome attitude toward sex, had some wise and sensible words concerning the sexual relations of husband and wife. Phillips' translation of the passage, which is plainer and more pointed than most, is as follows:

The husband should give his wife what is due to her as his wife, and the wife should be as fair to her husband. The wife has no longer full rights over her own person, but shares them with her husband. In the same way the husband shares his personal rights with his wife. Do not cheat each other of normal sexual intercourse, unless of course you both decide to abstain temporarily to make special opportunity for fasting and prayer. But afterward you should resume relations as before, or you will expose yourselves to the obvious temptation of the devil (1 Cor. 7:3-5, Phillips).

In commenting on this statement by Paul, Bailey says: "It is curious that this remarkable and pregnant concept should have had a negligible influence upon Christian thought—probably because it invests coitus with a significance which proved unacceptable in the face of rapidly developing ascetical tendencies in the Church."[1] Those ascetical tendencies came into the stream of the Christian movement from Greek rather than Hebrew thought.

While the Bible reveals that sex as such is a good gift of God to man, it also reveals that it is to be used in God-approved ways, in ways that will fulfill God's purposes. God's purpose evidently is that husbands and wives, through physical union, will find their fulfillment in one another, will have communication at the deepest level of their beings, will truly become one. The sexual union involves their total personalities. This is one reason why sex "must be practiced and controlled in such a manner that other functions of the Self are not thereby disturbed or hampered."[2] Another clearly stated purpose, one that it seems is subservient to the other, and possibly a result and an expression of the deeper purpose, is the propagation of the race.

When we remember the high purposes of God for sex, which he has restricted in its expression to the husband-wife relationship, it is no wonder that there are no sins more uniformly or harshly condemned in the Bible than those involving sex: homosexuality as well as fornication and adultery. Contemporary men and women, young and old, need to remember that these sins are sins against the eternal purposes of God and that one cannot violate the fundamental laws of God which are written into our natures and the nature of our world without paying the price for such violation.

THE ONE-FLESH CONCEPT

When Jesus said, "For this reason a man shall leave his father and mother, and be made one with his wife; and the two shall become one flesh" (Matt. 19:5, NEB), He was quoting Genesis 2:24. A study of the latter will reveal that "for this reason" refers back to the fact that man was created male and female. The love, the desire, the drive that leads men and women to form a new union is the deep desire to restore their original unity. They were created male and female, created for one another, they are incomplete until they are united with one another. This unity is not restored until husband and wife have had physical union with each other. This makes them "one flesh." Bailey sums it up as follows: "This means that through sexual intercourse in which they consummate their love, they restore the original pattern of human unity."[3]

Whatever the statement "and the two shall become one flesh" may mean, Jesus wanted to stress it since He stated it twice. He followed this twofold emphasis with a challenging word: "What God has joined together, man must not separate" (Matt. 19:6, NEB). The emphasis here is on "what God has joined." How does God join a husband and wife together? How is this union related to the one-flesh concept? What is meant by the "one-flesh" union? Does this refer exclusively to a physical union? Is the physical union an essential aspect of the one-flesh concept? Bailey states the matter adequately and compactly as follows: "Although the union in 'one flesh' is a physical union established by sexual intercourse . . . it involves at the same time the whole being and affects the personality at the deepest level."[4] This raises the sexual union of husband and wife above the lower orders of life. In the animal world there is a polarity of male and female. Among human beings it is a polarity between man and woman—between total personalities. This seems that while physical union makes a husband and wife one flesh, the one-flesh concept, in the deepest and fullest sense, involves much more than the strictly physical—it includes the total personality.

A question relating to the one-flesh union that is not easy to answer is: "Does every act of physical union with one of the opposite sex establish a one-flesh union?" The question or problem is deepened by Paul's statement in 1 Corinthians: "Do you not know that your bodies are limbs and organs of Christ? Shall I then take from Christ His bodily parts and make them over to a harlot? Never! You surely know that anyone who links himself with a harlot becomes physically one with her (for Scripture says, 'The pair shall become one flesh'); but he who links himself with Christ is one with him, spiritually" (1 Cor. 6:15-17, NEB).

We cannot and need not interpret this passage at any length. It does point out the seriousness of fornication. Even a relationship to a harlot, which means that one takes what belongs to Christ and joins it to her, forms in a sense and to a degree a one-flesh union. This is what Bailey labels as a false, invalid one-flesh union. In contrast,

> the true, authentic *henosis* is effected by intercourse following consent between a man and a woman who love one another and who act freely, deliberately, responsibly, and with the knowledge and approval of the community, and in so doing . . . conform to the Divine law.[5]

Every *henosis* or union which outwardly appears to be valid does not attain to the ideal set forth by Bailey. He recognizes that this is true. He suggests that there are marriages that are loveless or which because of some maladjustment fall below the ideal implied by "one flesh."

One wonders if there may not be an ideal here that can in one sense of the word be used to judge or evaluate not only the initial union of the husband and wife but also every subsequent union. At least the husband and wife should ask themselves the question: Is this the union of our total personalities? Does it measure up to God's highest demands of this area of our lives? These are questions of abiding relevance.

It is wise to remember that while the one-flesh union involves more than the body, the bodily or physical union is involved in the one-flesh concept. It is the physical union that basically makes the husband and wife one. This means that when Jesus said, "What God has joined together, man must not separate" He was referring to a joining together that basically involved a physical union. This type of joining together applies to non-Christians as well as Christians.

HUSBANDS AND WIVES

There are some biblical teachings of considerable significance in addition to those previously set forth concerning the relationships of husbands and wives. We shall examine a few of these.

For example, the emphasis in the Old Testament against intermarriage, when properly understood, has an abiding relevance (see Ex. 34:12-16; Deut. 7:1-8; Ezra 9:1). The relevance of the restrictions is related primarily to their purpose. This purpose is clearly revealed as follows: "You shall not make marriages with them, giving your daughters to their sons or taking their daughters for your sons. For they would turn away your sons from following me, to serve other gods; then the anger of the Lord would be kindled against you, and he would destroy you quickly" (Deut. 7:3-4). One author says that "the real and only purpose of this bar to marriage was to protect Israel from paganism."[6] He also says, "The generally accepted objection to intermarriage was . . . based purely upon religious grounds."[7]

We are persuaded that this is a continuing concern of our heavenly Father, and should be an abiding concern of the Christian church and the Christian home. It is Paul who plainly says, "Be not mismated with unbelievers" ["unequally yoked with unbelievers" ASV] (2 Cor. 6:14). A reading of the verses immediately following will rather clearly reveal that Paul is here stating a general principle rather than speaking specifically of marriage. However, "the most obvious application of such a prohibition would be to intermarry with the heathen."[8]

Whether or not the latter is a correct interpretation of 2 Corinthians 6:14, Paul is quite specific about the marriage of a widow. He says that "she is free to be married to whom she wishes, only in the Lord" (1 Cor. 7:39). *The New English Bible* has a rather unusual translation of the last portion of the preceding: "provided the marriage is within the Lord's fellowship." *The American Commentary* says that she could be married only to a Christian, while the *Expositor's Greek Testament* says that it forbids union with a heathen and then adds: "It also forbids any union formed with un-Christian motives and otherwise than under Christ's sanction."[9] If Paul would say that for a widow, he would certainly say it for all young people who are contemplating marriage. How many headaches and heartaches would be avoided in later life if Christian young people would follow the admonition of Paul!

The Bible also clearly reveals that God's original purpose and ultimate ideal for marriage is the joining together of one man and one woman as husband and wife for life (1 Cor. 7:39; Rom. 7:2-3). Any union that does not last until death falls short of God's purposes.

It may be wise to recall again Genesis 2:24: "Therefore a man leaves his father and his mother and cleaves to his wife, and they become one flesh." Parents and sons and daughters should know that when one marries, his or her supreme human loyalty from then until the end of life's journey belongs to the husband or the wife. This means that no in-law (or out-law) will be permitted to come between the husband and wife.

Another matter that needs to be examined from the biblical perspective is the relation of men and women in general, and in the home in particular. The Bible plainly says that in Christ there is neither male nor female (Gal. 3:28). Parenthetically, it might be said that the emphasis here is possibly primarily on unity rather than equality, although the unity in Christ which makes us one will tend to place us on the same level with all who are in the Christian fellowship. Within the early Christian fellowship there were several women who served effectively. Some of them traveled with Jesus and His disciples and ministered to them of

their substance (Luke 8:3; 23:27, 49, 55). Some women had relatively prominent places in the ministry of the churches. Along
with many others were Priscilla or Prisca, who was associated
with her husband in effective missionary endeavors (Acts 18:2;
Rom. 16:3; 1 Cor. 16:19), and Phoebe, a servant or deaconess
(RSV) of the church at Rome (Rom. 16:1).

There is another side, however, to the position given to women
in the church and in the home. They were definitely made subservient to men. It is possible that this emphasis stemmed to some
degree from the fear that women would exercise too freely the
freedom that they had in Christ. It seems that Paul was constantly
fearful that women and Christians in general would abuse the
new-found liberty they had.

Whatever may have been the reason, there is no question about
the fact that Paul counseled women to be submissive to men in the
church (1 Cor. 14:33-34; 1 Tim. 2:11-12) and to their husbands
in the home (Eph. 5:22-24). He plainly says that while Christ is
the head of everything, the man or the husband is head of the
woman (1 Cor. 11:3). An examination of this verse will reveal,
however, that this is no abject submission, the woman is to be
subordinate to the man as Christ is to God. It is a submission in
office or function of one who is essentially equal in nature. In
other words, the subordination of woman to man, whether in
the church or in the home, is to be the subordination of an equal
to an equal for the sake of order.

The subjection is spelled out very specifically in that wonderfully rich passage in Ephesians (5:21-33), which sets forth the
Christian ideal of marriage and the home. One commentator says
of this passage: "It is the loftiest conception of that relation that
has ever come from human pen."[10] Paul says, "Wives, be subject
to your husbands, as to the Lord." (The *Amplified New Testament* says "as [a service] to the Lord.") He says that the husband
is head of the wife as Christ is of the church, and just as the
church is subject to Christ, so the wife is to be to her husband.

The sharpness of this subjection may be relieved, to some degree, if we remember that Paul had just set forth the general principle that Christians should be in subjection to one another "out of reverence for Christ." He then applied this general principle in three areas—relation of wives to husbands, of children to parents, and of servants to masters. Peter (1 Pet. 3:1-2) says that the wife should be submissive even to a non-Christian husband, the motive being that such a husband might be won to the Lord.

Was this idea of submission of the woman and the wife an adjustment of the Christian ideal to the culture of the New Testament days, or does it represent God's abiding purpose in the relation of men and women? There can be no question about the biblical perspective: there is essential equality with distinctive functions and the man is to be the leader where the two are thrown into relations with one another.

How does this fit into a democratic society such as ours? What relevance does it have for family living in our day? It is our personal conviction that what we find in the Bible concerning the proper relation of men and women represents the abiding purpose or purposes of God. He has ordained that man shall be head of the house and that the wife should recognize that headship and fulfill her own distinctive functions in the home. It might be wise to remind ourselves that even in a democracy there are degrees of responsibility and distinctive functions to perform. The modern American home must be basically democratic, but unless there is to be chaos and anarchy, there must be some final source of authority in the home. The proper balancing of freedom and authority for parents, and also for children, will make for a happy relationship in the home and will help to build a home that will honor Christ and be a blessing to the members of the family and to the world. It is possible that some of the problems that we have in the contemporary home and even in our modern social order stem from the fact that men and women have been unwilling to accept and to fulfill their distinctive functions within the home and within society in general. We can be sure that any violation of God's order or purpose will lead to maladjustment and trouble in the home and in society.

Let us return for a brief look again at Ephesians 5. Paul, in this passage, places as great, and in some ways a more difficult, obligation upon the husband than upon the wife. The husband is to love his wife as himself, as his own body. He is to love her as Christ loved the church, and Christ loved the church enough to give His life for her. Few, if any, women would object to being in subjection to their husbands if those husbands loved them as Christ loved the church. And the word for love in this passage is that great New Testament word *agape*, which is a word so distinctive that some New Testament scholars do not believe it should have been translated. It represents a love that gives itself unselfishly to the object loved. This means that the husband's love for his wife, and hers for him, acquires a new meaning, a new depth, a new dimension. It partakes of the divine quality.

PARENTS AND CHILDREN

There are some valuable guidelines in the Bible for parents and children in their relations to one another.

Children should honor their parents, which is one of the Ten Commandments and which Paul said was the first commandment with a promise (Eph. 6:2). Jesus also cited the commandment in reprimanding the disciples of the Pharisees and the scribes for failing to care for their needy parents (Matt. 15:1-6).

Throughout the Bible, children are taught to obey their parents. Paul sums it up for us when he says, "Children, obey your parents in the Lord, for this is right" (Eph. 6:1). The phrase "in the Lord" creates some difficulty. Incidentally, it is not in some of the manuscripts and is not included in a few of the translations, such as Williams and the *New English Bible*. If "in the Lord" belongs in the passage, then Colossians, which closely parallels Ephesians, may help us to interpret it correctly. A somewhat similar verse in Colossians says, "Children, obey your parents in everything, for this pleases the Lord" (Col. 3:20). Paul is evidently counseling obedience in general. He is not saying, "Obey your parents if they are Christian," or "if what they ask you to do is in harmony with the will of the Lord." No, he is stating, as a general principle, that children should obey their parents.

There is at least one other biblical teaching concerning the relation of children to parents that may be and is needed in our day. Children are responsible for parents in real need.

This seems to have been the point of the reprimand referred to earlier of the Pharisees and scribes by Jesus. He said to them, "You have a fine way of rejecting the commandment of God, in order to keep your tradition!" He then quoted the commandment: "Honor your father and your mother" and reminded them that they said, "If a man tells his father or his mother, What you would have gained from me is Corban (that is, given to God)— then you no longer permit him to do anything for his father or mother, thus making void the word of God through your tradition which you hand on. And many such things you do" (see Mark 7:8-13).

There is a brief section in 1 Timothy that discusses "widows indeed" (ASV), "real widows" (RSV), or widows "in the full sense" (NEB). What is meant by "real widows"? An examination will reveal that it is closely related to the emphasis that we are making that children are to provide for their needy parents. This will be clearly indicated by quoting a couple of verses: "The status of widow is to be granted only to widows who are such in the full sense. But if a widow has children or grandchildren, then they should learn as their first duty to show a loyalty to the family and to repay what they owe to their parents and grand-parents; for this God approves" (1 Tim. 5:3-4, NEB). Notice the expression "to repay what they owe." Children are indebted to their parents. They are to pay back a part of that debt by caring for them when they are in need.

Again, possibly we should ask the question: Was this teaching or exhortation a result of the environment of that day or is it abidingly relevant? Does it apply in a day when we have private and government agencies and institutions to care for needy parents? My judgment is that it is just as relevant today as it was in the New Testament days, and that this obligation rests particularly heavy upon Christian children to care for their needy parents. Certainly, wisdom and sense need to be used. Parents should be encouraged to remain independent and self-reliant as long as possible, but it is a reflection upon us and our religion if they are cared for by others or by government agencies when we are able to do it ourselves. You will understand that I am not talking about social security, which is a type of insurance to which they have contributed.

Let us now turn the table and think of the relation of parents to children. We should always remember that the primary order of responsibility is the parent for the child rather than the child for the parent. Both Testaments emphasize the responsibility of parents to teach and to train their children. They are to teach them the commandments of God persistently, but first of all by walking in the way of those commandments themselves (see Deut. 6:1-9). Parents are also instructed to "train up a child in the way he should go, and when he is old he will not depart from it" (Prov. 22:6). Training involves teaching but it involves more than teaching. It is doubtful if anyone can train up a child in the way he ought to go unless he walks in that way himself. The idea of training involves to some degree a dedication of the child to the way he should go or according to his way, his individual way, or the way that God would have him to go. Notice the great promise in the latter part of the verse: "and when he is old ["and even when he is old" ASV] he will not depart from it."

One method of instruction which is stressed a great deal in the Bible is discipline. It may be true that in some of the passages in the Old Testament the discipline is rather harsh and hard, but the overall biblical emphasis should be considered seriously by contemporary parents. Entirely too many children in contemporary American homes are growing up largely undisciplined. Let us never forget that the undisciplined child is an unhappy child. He will tend to be a problem to his home, his school, his church, and the world, and even to himself.

Paul gives us a pointed word concerning the responsibility of parents to their children. He says, "Fathers, do not provoke your children to anger, but bring them up in the discipline and instruction of the Lord" (Eph. 6:4). Notice the combining of discipline and instruction. Instruction refers to teaching in general, and discipline is a method of instruction. Also notice the expression, "of the Lord." It is Christian training and discipline that is of Christ "proceeding from Him and prescribed by Him."[11] Christian parents should find in this statement encouragement and guidance in their relationship to their children.

THE CHURCH AND THE HOME

Let us say just a few words concerning the church and the home. In writing to Philemon, Paul sent greetings to him, to Apphia, evidently his wife, and to Archippus, who was doubtlessly their son, and to the church in their house. This idea of a church in a home is found elsewhere in Paul's greetings to Nymphas (Col. 4:15) and to that wonderful couple, Aquilla and Prisca or Priscilla (Rom. 16:5), and also from Aquilla and Priscilla and the church in their house to the church at Corinth (1 Cor. 16:19), where they had formerly lived.

This expression simply meant that a church or at least a portion of a church—an assembly or a congregation—met in the homes of those who were evidently prominent and influential members of the churches. There were no church buildings. The same thing is happening today on home and foreign mission fields.

It is possible, however, that this expression, "the church in your house," is somewhat symbolic of the relation between the Christian home and the Christian church. These two institutions belong together. The church is or should be a family permeated by the family spirit. The members of the church are brothers and sisters in Christ.

On the other hand, the Christian home is or should be an embryonic or at least a microscopic *ekklesia*, a small group of called out ones, called out from the world and called unto dedication to and fellowship with God and with one another. It has some distinctive functions, as is also true of the church, but it also shares some functions with the church, such as the evangelistic, the teaching, and the worship functions.

The two, church and home, should be laborers together in the work of God in the world. They both exist for the same big overall purpose: the promotion of the kingdom of God among men.

Chapter 6

THE FAMILY AND ITS AGING MEMBERS

What can we do about Mother, Dad, or in some cases Dad and Mother, or dear old Aunt Suzie or Uncle Jim? Questions such as these are being asked more frequently and are more perplexing, in many ways, than formerly. This is due, in the main, to the increasing number of older people and the more varied programs for the care of the aged.

We shall limit our discussion to the Christian family and its aged members, which means that there will be many problems related to the aged that we shall not consider. For example, we shall not appraise the provision of governmental agencies for the aged, including the present retirement programs and policies. We shall not discuss adult education which is of major importance in the total program for the aged. We will not give any consideration to more personal problems such as the remarriage of a widowed father or mother, or, to specialized problems such as caring for the mentally ill.

It may be wise to share with you that there is considerable personal experience that provides some background for this discussion. My mother was left a widow without any income for seventeen years after dad's death. My wife's mother, who lived to be ninety-five years old, was a widow for nineteen years and lived with us during the winters, sometimes as much as six to eight months, for seventeen years. I am not suggesting that our problem was particularly unique; there are many of you who have or have had similar experiences.

PRELIMINARY CONSIDERATIONS

Before proceeding with our discussion, let us set forth some figures and statistics that will point up the extent and nature of the general problem we face in our society. A chart book provided for the participants in the White House Conference on Aging a few years ago stated that the twentieth century has seen the number of older people in the nation increase fivefold, while the population as a whole increased only twofold. The word "older" refers to those sixty-five years of age and above.

Older people numbered 3,000,000 or 4 percent of the population in 1900. The number had increased to 16,000,000 in 1960 with a prediction of 20,000,000 by 1970. There are 3,800 Americans who turn sixty-five every day. Part of the increase in the number and percentage of older people is due to the noticeable increase in life expectancy. For women, this has been twenty years within the past fifty years.

It is rather interesting to note that the states with the smallest percentage of the population sixty-five years of age or over are all southern states except Arizona, New Mexico, Nevada, Utah, and Wyoming. The situation in the southern states may be largely due to the relatively high birth rate and hence the large number of children in those states.

Any real breakthrough in the discovery of a remedy or a prevention for two or three diseases, such as cancer or heart trouble, would send the life expectancy skyrocketing. The possibility of such discoveries means that the percentage of the aged in our population may sharply increase in the years ahead.

The chart book provided for the participants in the White

House Conference for Aging also revealed that most persons sixty-five and over have some regular income. The broadest program is O.A.S.I. (Old Age Survivor's Insurance), which is now paying benefits to nearly two out of three individuals in that age bracket. It was also revealed that over 70 percent of the OASI beneficiaries own their own homes, 87 percent of these are free of mortgages. A considerable percentage of the old people have some income from interest, rent, and dividends.

Another figure that is even more relevant for our purpose is the fact that 70 percent of the aged lived in their own homes, with an additional 21 percent with relatives, and only 6 percent in institutions. The others lived with individuals other than relatives.

One of the increasingly popular ways to care for the aged is in nursing homes. It is well to remember that the average age of patients in nursing homes is 80, with two-thirds of them over 75. Also, two-thirds of those in such homes are women and less than one-half of them can walk alone. Many are bed-ridden and mentally confused.

One of the most dynamic speakers at the White House Conference for the Aging was a Jewish rabbi and scholar (Abraham J. Heschel). He suggested that once we attain old age we consider it a defeat, "a form of capital punishment." Medical science is extending the years we can live and yet "we continue to act as if it were a disease." He suggested that "more money and time are spent on the art of concealing the signs of old age than on the art of healing heart disease and cancer." He further said that there are "more patients in the beauty parlors than in the hospitals. We would rather be bald than grey." He further suggested that monotheism has acquired a new meaning: "The one and only thing that counts is being young. Youth is our god, and being young is divine. . . . The cult of youth is idolatry." His own personal conclusion was: "Old age is not a defeat but a victory, not a punishment, but a privilege."[1]

NEEDS OF THE AGED

The aged need, in many cases, to reconstruct their own thinking. They need to recognize that growing old does not necessarily mean stagnation. There can be a sense in which growing old gives opportunities for growth, for new insights, for enriched experiences. The Jewish rabbi suggested that one should enter old age in the way a college student enters the senior year at his college or university. There is an exciting anticipation of the consummation of his training. As we grow old we need to be saved from the past and to live in the present. Quoting again from the rabbi: "All it takes to sanctify time is God, a soul, and a moment. And the three are always here."[2]

The basic needs of the aged are threefold: (1) somewhere to live, (2) something to do, and (3) someone to care. We shall spend quite a bit of time in later sections discussing where they may live. Let us never forget that the other needs are just as basic.

The aged need something to do. In other words, they need to be needed, whether they are living in their own home, in the home of relatives, or elsewhere. They need to feel that they are contributing something significant to the lives of others and to the world.

This is rather closely related to the need of the aged for independence. Children should be unusually careful that they never rush the season of dependency. "Loss of independence is a bitter pill to swallow, so the longer you can help your parents to enjoy the sweets of leading their own lives in their own way in their own pace, the better."[3]

We should never forget the third of those basic needs—the need to have someone to care. It has been suggested that two-thirds of the old people in the United States feel unwanted. The general attitude toward old age in our country is contradictory. Theoretically, we honor the aged, but in actuality we do not. Our attitude is often a negative one and at times even scornful. The attitude toward them may help explain why some old people become hard to get along with—they feel frustrated, unwanted. They need to be appreciated and loved.

This means, among other things, that children should count it a privilege to help care for them when there is a real need. It also means that as long as they live in their own home or at least away from the home of the children, they should be visited regularly. Furthermore, they should not be used as glorified, or what someone has called, "built-in" baby-sitters.

Here is someone's idea of a "Bill of Rights for Older People":

> The right to be treated as a person.
> The right to be treated as a grown-up.
> The right to have their say about their own life.
> The right to a fair chance on their merits.
> The right to a future.
> The right to have fun and companions.
> The right to be romantic.
> The right to the help of one's family in becoming
> interesting to that family.
> The right to professional help whenever necessary.
> The right to be old.'

There might be some of this that we would want to change, but at least these "rights" should be challenging to us.

GUIDING PRINCIPLES

Before we come specifically to methods of caring for needy parents, let us set forth several principles that should guide us in what we do for them.

1. We should do what we can do to dignify old age.

There are cultures in which the old are especially honored. This has been true in our own culture to a greater degree in the past than at the present. Respect for the aged is tied in rather definitely with the idea that wisdom comes with age. This is generally true. In an activistic society such as ours, we tend to honor and respect primarily those who can do things rather than those who are wise. This is one factor that creates problems for older people. The preceding does not mean to imply that all the aged are wise. Those who are wise tend to get wiser and the foolish to get more foolish, but certainly the attainment of real wisdom is the work of a lifetime.

2. It should be recognized that the primary responsibility for providing for the later years of life rests upon the individual himself.

Long before old age arrives, all of us should be planning for those years. Plans should be made for retirement, for methods to care for our own material needs. We should seek to avoid financial dependence upon our children. We should keep ourselves alert to what is going on in the world. We should also develop new interests as we mature and plan for continuing creative activities.

3. The preceding means that any program by the family or by private or governmental institutions for the aged should provide for or protect their independence in every conceivable way.

For example, if an aged individual is able, let him carry as much of his own financial load as possible, even if it means that he will pay board in his son's or daughter's home. If financial aid has to be given by the children, let them give it directly to the one in need and let him pay his own bills. This should be the procedure as long as possible. In other words, if we need to care for one or both of our parents, let us avoid the temptation to treat them as children. They do not want to be their children's "children." It is even possible that many church and governmental programs for adults are too exclusively childlike in their approach. Provision needs to be made for games and hobbies, but older people also need the opportunity to participate in things that they will consider creative and worthwhile.

4. If the aged are unable to care for themselves, then the responsibility for their care rests first of all upon the members of the family.

Children honor their fathers and mothers by caring for them when they are in need. Let us repeat, however, that they should not be in too big a hurry to do this. They should help their parents to maintain their independence as long as feasible. It should be remembered, however, that children have an obligation to their parents. A father and mother may find it possible to sustain a dozen children, while, unfortunately, frequently the dozen children think it is impossible to care for one father or mother. The provision for a parent by children should be considered a privilege and never looked on as charity. They should be cared for in such a way as to maintain their dignity and self-respect.

One real test of the character of a son or daughter, or even of a society, is the attitude toward the aged. It is comparatively easy to love children, it is more difficult many times to love the aged, the crippled, the dependent. The ability to do this not only is a test of character but it also reveals how much the spirit of Christ has permeated our lives.

5. The care for needy parents should be shared by all the children.

In some cases, of course, there is only one child and that one will have to carry the entire load. Where there are multiple children, an attempt should be made to see that all share in the caring for the aged parent or parents. This should be done for the sake of the aged themselves but also for the sake of the sons and daughters. One son or daughter should be careful not to usurp the responsibilities and even the prerogatives of the other members of the family. There may be a need in many cases for a family caucus to work out a program to care for the needy parents. It is recognized that in many homes the children cannot share equally. They will have differing family situations. But let us remember that the basic principle is that it should be a shared responsibility.

6. In caring for needy parents or other relatives, as suggested previously, they should be kept in their own homes as long as possible.

The home is a man's castle, as much at 84 as at 24, and "when anyone must leave his castle something besides his body is liable to move out, too."[5] Unless there exists an extreme health or financial problem, living with any of the children, generally speaking, should be avoided as long as possible.

7. One other guiding principle is to remember, when you are working out a program for a needy aged member of the family, that it may be a long-term job.

For example, my wife's mother lived to be 95, with two of her sisters living to be older than she. One may expect an arrangement to last only three to five years and discover that it will continue for twenty to twenty-five years.

CARING FOR THE AGED OUTSIDE THEIR OWN HOMES

In this and the next section we are assuming that aged parents or other relatives must be cared for in some way outside of their own homes.

Let us repeat, however, that if at all possible, take care of them in their own home. This may mean that the children will have to contribute to their support. It is possible that some relative, boarder, or housekeeper will need to move in and help care for them. It may be that a housekeeper on a part-time basis could provide all that is needed in the way of assistance. Or, someone might come in once or twice a week to clean house and to do the heavier work about the place. If there is room in the house, it might be that a family could move in and share the house with the aged individual or individuals.

If aged parents remain in their own home there will be a need for some special arrangements, such as a telephone close by the bed where they can call neighbors or a member of the family when an emergency arises. Some provision may need to be made to get them to church regularly. This might be by members of the family, by neighbors, or even by taxi. In planning for them, be careful about forcing things upon them.

There are a number of ways that the aged can be cared for other than in the homes of children or relatives. There are apartment hotels for those who can afford them. In practically all cities there are numbers of old people who live in these hotels. There are nursing and convalescent homes—a few of these are sponsored by churches or denominations. Whether or not it is wise to put an aged individual in such a home will largely depend on the individual. A missionary's mother is in a denominationally supported home and says she is as happy as she would be anywhere. There are other older people who would not go or should not go to a home. They would feel that they were being shunted away and would not live long. We can no more generalize about the aged than we can about children, youth, or the middle ages.

If it seems wise or best to place the aged in a rest or nursing home, the children have a responsibility to help in its selection. Among other things, they will need to consider the financial arrangements, the medical and nursing services available, the background of the people in the home, the opportunities for recreation, for reading, for expression of personal likes and dislikes, such as having a private room that they can arrange somewhat as they like. They will need to investigate the opportunities for creative service for those who are able to do something about the home. If a father and mother are left together, will they have the opportunity of living together? Certainly if parents are put in a home, the children should visit them regularly and should have the parents frequently visit in their homes.

There are a number of factors in addition to those previously mentioned that would help to determine where and how aged parents should be cared for. Without spelling these out, let us never forget that the children have the primary responsibility to see that their parents are cared for adequately. If it seems wise or best to place them in a home, let us do it, but let us be sure that we are not doing it just to get rid of them.

There are other things that will help to determine what we should do about aged parents. The decision will need to be made on the basis of what we can do, and not necessarily on what we would like to do or what others think we should do. Some questions that will help us in reaching a decision are the following: What will our parents let us do for them? How much can they do for themselves? What can they afford, and what can we afford to do?

Let us repeat that we should consider the personality and the background of each individual. How will he or she react to what we are contemplating? One factor that will determine that is where they have lived. For example, have they lived all their lives in a big house on a farm? On the other hand, are we living in an apartment in the city? Have they lived in one place all of their lives? Are we with a firm or in a business or profession that requires frequent moves? We can visualize some of the problems that would be created if situations implied by the preceding questions existed. All of this means that what might be wise for one family to do might be very unwise for another. Let us repeat, however, that this in no way relieves the children of their responsibility. Some way, somehow, they are to care for their needy parents.

CARING FOR THE AGED IN THE HOME

If an aged relative needs to be cared for in the home, we may need to decide whether to live in their home or for them to live in our home. There are some advantages from their perspective in living in their own home. They are in familiar surroundings; they tend to cling to and prize old furnishings. It is harder for them to make adjustments than for those who are younger. But on the other hand, there are also some potential problems. They will tend to have or to develop a parent-child attitude and relationship again, or they may tend to be host and/or hostess to the members of their own family. From the viewpoint of a son or a daughter, there are many advantages in having aged parents come to live with them rather than living in the parental home. This will be best in the vast majority of the cases. It is recognized that in many cases the children have no choice in the matter: because of their work they do not and cannot live in the same community as their parents.

Although it may be necessary to have them live in our home, it should be recognized that no house is big enough for two families, particularly when those families are related. This means that we and they should recognize ahead of time that there will be some problems. Regardless of how good and kind and considerate grandmother and grandfather have always been in their home, they cannot and will not be exactly the same in someone else's home. They are not living in a normal situation. There is a strain on them as well as on their children and grandchildren.

There are a number of specific problems that arise when such a living arrangement is necessary. The husband and wife should recognize that considerable privacy will have to be sacrificed. There will also be differences at times about such simple but sometimes aggravating things as the temperature of the house, the proper ventilation, and special foods and diets. The bathroom can create rather serious problems and friction. Frequently, the father and the children are in a hurry in the morning to get off to work and to school. This will mean that grandfather or grandmother should give them priority. If at all possible, a separate bath for grandfather or grandmother would be a wise provision. Problems tend to become particularly perplexing where there are children in the home. The grandparents may be either captious and fussy or doting. Sometimes the latter is compensation for having been too hard on their own children. The problems with grandchildren tend to be aggravated when they get into the teens.

It may be wise to have an understanding about a number of things before the aged father or mother comes into the home to live. This is particularly important concerning the children. The discipline of the children should be left to the parents and not to the grandparents, except in cases where the latter provide most of the care for the grandchildren. At least, children need to know who is the supreme court.

A positive approach should be made in caring for the aged in our home. We should see, if possible, that they have some useful task to perform. They should have their own room (or rooms) with the responsibility of caring for it and arranging it as they desire. This is particularly important for grandmother. If possible, have familiar furnishings. If this cannot be done, have something in there that will be unusually attractive and comfortable for an old person, and which will become recognized in the household as belonging to the grandparent.

We should seek to get the aged members of the family into the life of the church and the community. This means regular attendance at Sunday school, church, and related groups. They should be encouraged to correspond with old friends back in the home community, while they cultivate new friends in the new community. It would be wise to take them back "home" occasionally to visit with their old friends.

Rather than the aged being shifted around to all the children, there should be at least one place that is considered home or headquarters. They may spend as much time with the other sons and daughters as they do at "home," but such an arrangement will give them a sense of security and stablility.

If they are entirely dependent financially, the children should see that they have sufficient spending money for clothes, incidentals, and church offerings.

With all of the potential problems that may arise when aged members of the family have to live in the home of a son or a daughter, the family can be unified. Just as a cake having three layers is one cake, so a family with three generations can be one unified family. There can be real blessings to all concerned in the associations of the old and the young. It can be an enriching experience for grandparents, parents, and grandchildren. Many homes can testify that this can be true and has been true in their own personal experiences.

Chapter 7

THE CHURCHES AND DIVORCE

David Mace tells a rather revealing and disturbing incident that happened at the close of a lecture he delivered to a packed house in Ceylon. The subject of the lecture had been "Marriage in the Modern World." At the close he was challenged by "a dark-skinned gentleman in flowing white robes." The man came to the platform and read from a crumbled piece of paper some facts and figures for the United States concerning divorce, juvenile delinquency, sexual crimes, and related matters. He then addressed the audience as follows: "Ladies and gentlemen, that is how they are living in the part of the world from which our lecturer comes. Do you think that people who behave like that have anything to teach us about how to conduct our family relationships?"[1]

This incident reveals that the problem of divorce is not only a problem for pastors and churches but also for our nation, for the representatives of our nation, and the cause of Christ around the world.

The present discussion of the problem will be presented under the following major headings: (1) The Contemporary Situation, (2) The Biblical Perspective, and (3) Continuing Problems.

THE CONTEMPORARY SITUATION

In painting the picture concerning the contemporary situation regarding divorce we shall limit ourselves to the United States. In general, there has been a continuing increase in the number of divorces and in the divorce rate. There have been some fluctuations in the movement, but these have not affected the overall trend. For example, divorces tend to increase after a war and to decline in a period of depression, but the number of divorces during the Great Depression never declined to the pre-World War I level.

The recording of divorces by the Census Bureau began in 1890 when there were 33,461 divorces in the United States. There were 100,000 divorces for the first time in 1914, with the number increasing to 200,000 fourteen years later in 1928. There was a decline during the Depression period, hitting a low of 164,241 in 1932, but the number went back over 200,000 in 1934. Eight years later, in 1942, the number had increased to more than 300,000 (321,000). There was a rapid increase after that, with 400,000 divorces in 1944, 485,000 in 1945, and the highest number in the history of our nation, 610,000, in 1946. There was then a noticeable drop to 483,000 in 1947 and 408,000 in 1948. In 1949 the number dropped below 400,000 (397,000) for the first time since 1944. Since that time, the number of divorces annually has leveled off at the rather high figure of 350,000-400,000 per year.

The large number of divorces and the high divorce rate in the United States is an indication and a symbol of the instability of the American home. In addition to those who had been divorced, the Federal Census Bureau recently revealed that one and three-quarter million husbands and wives were living apart because of marital discord. David Mace says that 20 percent of those who are living together are definitely unhappy, with another 35 percent not entirely happy. His conclusion is that "the average married couple in the United States today have less than a 50-50 chance of being happy in their life together."[2]

There are many factors contributing to the instability of the American home and to the attendant high divorce rate. One of these factors, which relates directly and indirectly to many other problems of the American home and to American life in general, is the shift from a predominantly patriarchal to a democratic type of home. This shift was more or less inevitable. Since the family is quite responsive to its environment, it could not help but be affected by the democratic conception of political life within our nation. Some of the problems of the modern American home stem from a misinterpretation of democracy itself. There is a failure to understand the difference between democracy and anarchy. The latter comes close to describing the situation in many American homes. There is little recognition of authority or of those who should exercise that authority. There is a tendency to consider authority undemocratic. In the home this lack of authority means theoretically that everyone is boss, but as Gibson Winter says, "We may be allergic to authority, but we cannot escape it."[3] One hopeful sign is that psychologists, psychiatrists, and others are beginning to see that the child needs order and authority, a thing that our grandparents and even most of our parents seemed to have known instinctively.

One of the reasons for the breakdown of authority in so many homes is the shifting, the mixing, or at best the uncertainty of the roles of husbands and wives, fathers and mothers. For example, the rights of the husband and father have decreased and his responsibilities have increased. Insofar as he plays a distinct role, it tends to be as much the mother role as the father role. For example, in the rearing of the children, wisely or unwisely, he performs many functions that belonged entirely to the mother of a generation or two ago. The children tend to ascribe to him quite a bit of the mother image. In contrast, the mother's rights in general have increased while her responsibilities have decreased. This helps to explain her freedom to work outside of the home. In turn, her working outside of the home has contributed to the changing of her role and also of her husband's role in the home.

Some students of the family are now saying that women lose as much as men when they fail to fulfill their distinctive roles in the home and in society in general. They suggest that the nature of woman demands a man who will be head of the household, exercising that headship, however, in such a way as to maintain the basic democratic framework. After all, even in an effective democracy there must be some distribution of responsibility. The idea of inequality within the home stands side by side with and balances the idea of basic equality.

It is unavoidable that our churches would be affected by the problem of divorce. Many church members have been divorced. Pastors know that if and when they speak concerning divorce, they will be speaking to the divorced and to many others who have members of their families who have been divorced. Some of these people will be among the most prominent and influential in the church. Sunday school teachers frequently face the same problem. This is enough to show that the contemporary problem of divorce reaches into our churches. What can and should our churches do about the problem? The first step in an answer is a study of the biblical perspective.

THE BIBLICAL PERSPECTIVE

Protestants generally have a deep reverence for the Bible. Most of them still believe that it is the chief tangible objective source for the will of God. Where it speaks specifically and plainly, its word is considered authoritative. There is, however, comparatively little of a specific nature set forth in the Scriptures concerning divorce. This forces us to depend, to a large degree, on the leadership of the Holy Spirit in determining what is right in the whole area of divorce. Let us hope and pray that we and the people in our churches will have the Spirit's leadership as we seek to know the Divine will concerning this and closely related problems. We need His guidance as we read, interpret, and apply the Scriptures to the problem.

There are a number of difficulties that face us. Some of the more important ones, most of which cannot be discussed, are as follows:

1. Nowhere in the Bible is there a systematic discussion of divorce; nowhere is a clear doctrine of divorce set forth. This means that from the biblical perspective there are many unanswered questions regarding divorce.

2. The fullest statements by Jesus (Mark 10 and Matthew 19) and by Paul (1 Corinthians 7) were in reply to specific questions, and in the case of the latter we do not even know the questions that had been asked. There is no way to know for sure how Jesus or Paul would have answered some of the contemporary questions concerning divorce.

3. How can we explain the difference in the order and content of Mark's and Matthew's account of the same incident, with its teachings on divorce? In particular, how can we explain the exception clause ("except for unchastity") in Matthew 19:9, which is also found in Matthew 5:32, or its absence in Mark?

4. Similarly, how can the teachings of Paul in 1 Corinthians 7:10-11 be made compatible with the teachings of Jesus as recorded in Matthew?

These are only a few of the difficulties, but they are enough to point up some of the very real problems we face in interpreting the teachings of the Bible concerning divorce and remarriage. The problems are of such significance, and the differences in the answers by competent authorities vary so much, that it should cause all of us to speak with some degree of humility, if not with hesitancy, regarding these matters.

In our discussion we shall restrict ourselves almost exclusively to the teachings of Jesus as found in Mark 10:2-12 and Matthew 19:3-12. This limitation means, among other things, that we shall make no attempt to consider the Old Testament teachings on divorce (Deut. 24:1-4; 22:13-19, 28-29; Lev. 21:7, 14; Ezek.

44:22; Mal. 2:16) nor the teachings of Paul (1 Cor. 7:10-16, if this refers to divorce), some of which are of real importance.

As suggested earlier, what Jesus said in Mark 10 and Matthew 19 regarding divorce was in response to a question by the Pharisees. Their question was, "Is it lawful for a man to divorce his wife?" (Mark 10:2), or, "Is it lawful to divorce one's wife for any cause?" (Matt. 19:3). The background for the question was evidently a difference in the interpretation of Deuteronomy 24:1 by two leading rabbis (Hillel—the liberal school, and Shammai—the strict school) and their followers. Time will not permit a detailed interpretation of the passages. About all we can do and want to do is to point out some directions for a correct interpretation.

Most interpreters of the teachings of Jesus on divorce have focused too exclusively on His statement or statements concerning divorce, remarriage, and adultery. These matters are abidingly interesting, but there is nothing of more significance in this conversation of Jesus with the Pharisees than the fact that He went back of the law and the interpretation of the law to God the Lawgiver and to His original purpose for the relation of husband and wife. Jesus said that in the beginning God created them male and female, and implied that there was no provision in God's original purpose for divorce. His plan was one man and one woman joined together as husband and wife for life. It was for this reason that a man would leave his father and mother and cleave to his wife and the two would become one, or one flesh.[4] Anything that violates or falls short of God's original purpose for marriage is a violation of God's basic law for the union of husband and wife, and hence it is sin. In other words, sin is involved, in some way and to some degree, in any divorce. This is basic and important in the biblical perspective concerning divorce. This does not mean, however, that divorce, whatever its basis, is an unpardonable sin. The sin that leads to divorce and that may be directly involved in divorce itself can be forgiven as is true of any other sin. This is not to treat the sin of divorce lightly. It is merely to place it in proper perspective and to give the power of God to forgive its rightful place.

A frequent question concerning the teachings of Jesus on marriage and divorce is whether or not He intended to speak as a lawgiver or as a teacher of moral ideals. Elsewhere, He seemed to be satisfied to set forth general principles. Did He change His approach and enunciate a law regarding divorce and remarriage?

Cole sums up his position regarding the whole matter as follows:

> To seek to make any of Jesus' absolutes into laws governing human behavior is to miss the whole point of his message, to erect a new legalism. He always gave concrete human need precedence over abstract ritual law. Man was not made for the Sabbath, nor for marriage as a prison. Both were rather made for man.[5]

Whether or not Jesus legislated concerning divorce and remarriage may not be as important as it first appears.

It has been suggested previously that the violation of the one-flesh union is a sin, since it is contrary to God's basic purpose for the home. It is also true that the fundamental principles of Jesus were and are in harmony with the basic laws of God, laws that are written into the nature of men and women and the home. In turn, this means that whether Jesus was legislating or not when He spoke of marriage and divorce does not make, in one sense, a great deal of difference. There is in divorce a violation of the basic purposes of God and hence, as suggested formerly, sin is involved. This is true of any divorce. The only difference in divorce on various bases is the nature of that sin.

We know, for example, that Jesus said that when one puts away his wife for any cause except fornication and marries another he commits the sin of adultery. There are, however, at least two rather perplexing questions concerning this sin: (1) Is the sin in such a divorce restricted to the one who puts away his wife and marries another, or is it possible that the so-called innocent party is also guilty, at least to some degree, of the sin that destroyed the one-flesh union? (2) Is the sin of adultery in such a case a perpetual or continuing sin, or does it involve a sin, one-act or otherwise, that can be forgiven by the Lord as is true of other sins?

The preceding discussion suggests that divorce can be considered a very serious matter without making a legalistic approach to the interpretation of the teachings of Jesus regarding divorce. In the light of a nonlegalistic approach it might be proper to ask a question about some husbands and wives who never divorce. Is it possible for a couple to remain together and yet for the union to have been basically destroyed? In other words, is it possible for married couples to destroy the deeper meaning of the one-flesh union and hence sin against the purposes of God for their union, although they continue to live together?

Let us raise again, but more specifically, the searching question and one that is not easy to answer: Should we be legalistic or nonlegalistic in our interpretation of the teachings of Jesus regarding divorce? Ebbie Smith, to whom I am indebted for a number of things in this chapter, suggests that the "main contention of those who foster the non-legalistic interpretation . . . is that the Christian ethic should present a way rather than a code." He further says that "the Christian spirit consists not in keeping stricter rules, nor in keeping rules better, but in not needing rules at all."[6] While this is true, it may be rather idealistic. The Christian way of life is basically an inner, vital relation with a Divine Person, and it will cause us to want to know and do His will; but we are imperfect and immature and hence we continue to make many mistakes. All of this means that there are some dangers in the strictly nonlegalistic as well as in the legalistic approach to marriage and divorce and to the Christian life in general.

The dangers of the nonlegalistic approach can be overcome, to some degree, by recognizing that the dissolution of marriage involves sin. Many of the nonlegalists agree that this is true. Some of them contend that divorce at times may be the lesser of two evils, just as is true of participation in war. For them "divorce may represent the only possible solution to some situations, a more creative and constructive alternative than a sterile and corrosive marriage."[7]

We can be sure "that true marriage is not preserved by form or force, by law or doctrine. . . . The marriage that has failed functionally cannot be made to succeed merely by preserving it structurally."[8] If the inner unity of marriage has been destroyed, if love is gone, there can be no meaningful union left. What is left is only legalized cohabitation, which may be little better than legalized adultery.

Let us repeat that this does not necessarily lead to an easy-going or lax attitude toward divorce. We should constantly remember that there is no divorce without sin, and often the sin is the entering of marriage lightly and hurriedly. Neither would this attitude justify a hurried divorce and/or remarriage. Every possible effort should be made to preserve the marriage, to restore or to create the conditions for a real and meaningful union. Since sin is involved in divorce, repentance and forgiveness can frequently prevent a divorce. When a divorce has occurred there should be a spirit of true repentance and forgiveness. Remarriage should not be considered at all without such a spirit.

CONTINUING PROBLEMS

In addition to the problems regarding the teachings of the Scriptures, there are a number of other contemporary problems in the whole area of marriage, divorce, and remarriage. Some of the more perplexing of these will be set forth largely through a series of questions. Occasionally, an answer will be given. The question method is used deliberately in this section with the hope that it will create some discussion.

1. Problems relating to those who are contemplating divorce.

Are they justified in getting a divorce? What is the basis on which they should make this decision? Even if they have the so-called scriptural grounds for divorce, is divorce the wisest or the most Christian solution for their problems? Have they sought consistently and persistently to find a solution for their difficulties? Do they recognize that divorce involves sin? Are they approaching the whole matter seriously and prayerfully? Have they faced up to their responsibility for the situation? Is there a genuine sense of repentance as well as a spirit of forgiveness? Have they considered as much as they should the effects of divorce, not only on themselves but also on their companion, the children, loved ones, church, community, and the cause of Christ.

What is the responsibility of a counselor? Should he ever be judgmental? Should he use the directive or the non-directive method of counseling? Should he ever categorically say that one is justified or not justified in getting a divorce, or must this be an individual decision? Can those of us who approach life's problems from the Christian perspective point the disturbed to a source of grace, strength, and guidance?

2. Problems of those who have been divorced.

A major question: Is it permissible for them to remarry? A few additional questions that may help them make their own decision: Have they genuinely repented of the sin that destroyed their union and led to a divorce? Have they recognized and do they recognize their responsibility for the former failure? Have they learned through their experiences? Is there a spirit of forgiveness toward the husband or wife who is involved in the former failure? As Christians, has the will of God been sought carefully and prayerfully?

Other possible questions: What are the motives for marrying again? What will be its effects on all concerned including the children if there are any, the family, the church? What about the other individual who might be involved in a possible marriage: his background, character, and so forth? How much of a chance for a really successful home is there?

3. Problems of those who have been divorced and remarried.

Sometimes they are plagued with some persistently disturbing questions. Most, but not all, of their problems evolve around the matter of adultery. If adultery by their former mate was not the real reason for the divorce, are they living in adultery with the present mate? If they are convinced that they are, what can they do about it?

4. The church and the divorced.

What should be the position of the church regarding the divorced? Should the church ever withdraw fellowship from them? Should they be accepted into the full fellowship of the church? Should there be any restrictions on their participation in the leadership of the church? For example, should a divorced man ever be ordained as a deacon, as a preacher?

What should be the attitude of church members toward the divorced? Is there a tendency on the part of some church members to manifest a self-righteous attitude toward the divorced?

Can the church and members of the church have a "Christian attitude" toward the divorced without leaving the impression, particularly with young people, that whether or not one is divorced makes little difference?

5. The pastor and the divorced.

We shall restrict ourselves to the difficult question about performing the ceremony for those who have been divorced. There are four rather clearly defined positions now maintained by pastors:

(1) Perform the ceremony for any who come with a license from the state, the idea being that the minister is simply serving as an agent of the state when he performs the ceremony.

(2) Consider each as an individual case. Those who maintain this position do not establish any formal basis on which they will make the decision about performing the ceremony. They ordinarily require at least one and in some cases more than one conference with the couple. The decision is made on the basis of whether or not they believe that the contemplated marriage has a good chance of becoming a sound Christian home.

(3) Those who will perform the ceremony only for those who have, from their perspective, the scriptural grounds for divorce. Most pastors who take this position will accept the word of the individual or individuals involved. Occasionally a pastor requires some proof.

(4) Those who will not perform the ceremony for any who have been divorced. Some of the pastors who practice this policy do not believe that the Scriptures would justify remarriage. Others take the position from a strictly practical viewpoint.

It might be said that whatever position one takes as a pastor he will find it difficult to maintain it consistently.

There are at least two other basic problems relating to divorce that should be given some attention:

6. Divorce and the individual conscience.

Whatever may be our position on divorce, it should be possible for us to maintain it and at the same time to defend the basic concept of the competency of the individual soul. The child of God should be led to see that he is personally responsible for whatever decision he makes regarding divorce and remarriage. It is not his pastor's responsibility to tell him what he can and cannot do. The pastor can and should help him to think through and evaluate objectively the possible problems that may be ahead for him.

On the other hand, the pastor has a personal responsibility to decide what he should do regarding the marriage ceremony for those who have been divorced. Members of the church ought to see that it would be just as wrong for them to expect the pastor to violate his conscience as for him to expect to be a conscience for them. Possibly it should also be said that the church has a responsibility to decide for itself what it shall do about electing divorced individuals to certain places of leadership in the life of the church.

7. The most effective approach to the problem of divorce.

The most effective approach to the divorce problem will not be a direct frontal attack on divorce by the church and church leaders. It would be far more effective to promote a preventive program, seeking to prepare young people for a wise choice of a companion, and attempting to give to them a sound basis for the founding and growth of a real Christian home. Every possible agency and channel should be used in this program: preaching, teaching, personal and group counseling, conferences, study courses, church library, and so forth.

Chapter 8

AMERICAN CULTURE AND TRADITIONAL CONCEPTS OF MARRIAGE

How would you define the words used in the subject?

"Marriage" will be interpreted as inclusive of all the activities and relationships of the home.

"Concepts" are ideas or opinions. When coupled with "traditional," they may properly be considered as norms or standards. While the term "traditional concepts" does not mean that those concepts have been universally accepted, they have been generally enough accepted to become an integral part of the culture.

The use of "traditional" as a prefix for "concepts" does not necessarily mean that those concepts no longer exist. We shall conclude, however, that they have been more generally accepted as norms or standards in the past than at the present time. There is a tendency for concepts or ideas to persist in theory long after they have ceased to be effective formative factors in daily practice. When this happens, those concepts, sooner or later, will be revised or rejected entirely. Such a revision or rejection may be both a result of and a factor in a changing culture.

The term "culture" has been defined in various ways. Christopher Dawson defines it as "a common social way of life—a way of life with a tradition behind it."[1] T. S. Eliot says that culture is "the way of life of a particular people living together in one place."[2] This place may be a neighborhood, a city, a region, a nation, or even a community of nations—anywhere where there is a common way of life. A more extensive culture is embodied in institutions: educational, political, social, and religious; it expresses itself in and through art, philosophy, science, and religion, as well as in concepts, values, customs, and habits. It is inclusive of everything that makes up its distinctive way of life.

It is hoped that this discussion will be sound from the viewpoint of the social sciences. However, it is assumed that we approach such a study primarily as servants of Christ and of our fellowmen. We represent different facets of the life and work of our churches. Consequently, our purpose here is to speak primarily from the perspective of our Christian faith.

This means, among other things, that we shall not be satisfied to be exclusively descriptive, but we shall endeavor at times to be evaluative. In other words, we are concerned with what ought to be as well as what is.

THE CHURCH, THE CULTURE, AND THE HOME

The close relation of the Christian faith to the culture as well as to the home justifies, if it does not make necessary, a brief statement concerning the relation of the church and culture. For example, the "traditional concepts of marriage" in our culture have been considerably influenced by the Christian religion.

Historically, there has been a close relation between the church—organized Christianity—and culture in Western civilization and in the United States in particular. They have influenced one another. There has been to some degree a mutual penetration. Paul Tillich says that "the church and culture are within, or along-side, each other." He adds, "The Kingdom of God includes both while transcending both."[3] This means, among other things, that Christian groups have made an impact on our

American culture, while, in turn, that culture has made an impact on those Christian groups.

This mutual penetration or two-directional influence of church and culture stems, to a degree, from the nature of the Christian church. In its organizational expression, it is a divine-human institution. It is divine in its origin, mission, and message. Its mission is performed and its message delivered, however, to men and women with their limitations and sins who live in a particular environmental situation. As Berger suggests, "Just as Christ was incarnate in human flesh, so the Church is always imbedded in the relativities of specific cultural situations."[4] The divine nature of the church, however, constantly stands in judgment against the church's adjustment or accommodation to the culture as a human institution. Its divine nature calls for the reformation or transformation, if not the actual condemnation, of the culture.

The church, in a sense, has a twofold function to perform in relation to the culture. It is an instrument of the culture, providing to some degree direction and cohesion for the culture. On the other hand, it stands or should stand in a prophetic relationship to the culture. These two seemingly contradictory functions of the church must be kept in proper balance if it is to make its maximum contribution to the culture. In other words, there is a sense in which the church stands within culture, but it must also stand apart from culture if it is to speak effectively God's message to the culture. The greater danger to the contemporary church is that it will get its message from the culture rather than speak a distinctive word to the culture. An important element in the message that the church should speak is what it would say concerning and to the Christian home.

Like the church, the Christian home is a divine-human institution. While as a human institution it cannot escape its environment or avoid entirely the impact of the surrounding culture, as a divine institution it should recognize a higher source of authority than the culture. The inner struggle between the human and divine elements in the church, and to a lesser degree in the Christian home, creates an inevitable tension. However, this tension is necessary if the church and the Christian home are to make the contribution they should to the culture.

Possibly a brief additional word should be said concerning the reduced influence of the church in our culture, which, in turn, has made a tremendous impact on the home. Partly because of its earlier success, as Winthrop Hudson suggests,[5] the church became proud of its influence on our culture, relaxed and made its peace with the world. A process which began with a culture largely molded by the Christian faith has ended with a church largely molded by the national culture. Complacent churches, to a distressing degree, have embraced the world. Such churches cannot speak an effective or an authoritative word to the world or to the institutions of the world. They do not, in the main, speak as one having authority even to those within their own fellowship.

Really, our American culture is no longer religiously informed unless we consider secularism a religion. Secularism, which is the ordering and conducting of life as if God does not exist, permeates and dominates our way of life. As Samuel Miller says, "The secular age . . . proclaims itself frankly, proudly, even a bit boisterously."[6]

Materialism, which is a product if not an integral part of secularism, also threatens our traditional values. Progress of the family, the community, the nation, and even the church is measured largely in material terms. For example, the status of the family is dependent not so much on the quality of family life maintained, nor the basic character of the members of the family, but on the type of house and community in which the family lives, the number and make of cars they drive, and other materially measured symbols. This represents a rather drastic change from the values of our rurally oriented society of a generation or two ago.

CONTEMPORARY AMERICAN CULTURE AND THE FAMILY

One of the most evident and drastic changes in America has been the shift from a predominantly rural to an urbanized culture. Marty suggests that the social revolution connected with urbanization is "the maturation and culmination of a century-long process whose psychic and spiritual effects are now for the first time being fully realized for America as a whole."[7] Those effects are as pronounced on the family as on any social institution. Gibson Winter says that "nothing is escaping the urban octopus, least of all the traditional patterns of the American family." He also says that "a new kind of family is slowly forming under the pressure of this threatening city life. . . . The city fashions families to suit its taste—families that can survive in an impersonal, anonymous jungle."[8] Many of those families are moving out from the central city to the suburbs and the satellite towns. But the cities persistently follow them, forcing them in many cases further and further out. And regardless of where they live, they cannot escape the impact of the city.

The homes of the suburbs and the satellite towns face some distinctive problems. As families are pushed further out, it takes increasing time for the father to commute to his work, resulting in less time with the family. This is one of the factors in the changing status of the father in the home. Also, frequently the mother thinks it is wise or necessary for her to work. This tends to create problems for her, her husband, and her children.

Even the towns and rural areas far removed from the cities cannot get away from the impact of urban life. The mass media of communication are used by the cities to dominate our culture. "It would be difficult to think of a single facet of America not shaped in whole or part by the mental climate of the metropolis."[9] Both rural styles of dress and patterns of thought are controlled largely by urban areas. The rural ethos dominant in the past is largely a thing of the past. In no area is this more evident than in our traditional concepts of marriage and the home.

The increased mobility of the American people, which is closely related to urbanization, is another factor that has influenced our traditional concepts of marriage and the home. This mobility expresses itself in many ways. There is a movement from the rural areas, the villages, and the towns to the cities. There is considerable movement from one section or region of the country to another. Then there is the movement out from the inner city.

Some of this mobility, which might be described as *horizontal,* is actually the result of a *vertical* mobility. The head of the house moves up the ladder of success in his chosen vocation or profession. This frequently requires a move to a new community. It helps to explain the tendency to move into a so-called better neighborhood, or into a more expensive house in the same community.

The mobility of the contemporary home frequently is disruptive to the home and creates problems for members of the family, particularly for the children. There is little sense of permanence and security, which represent basic needs of the maturing child. In contrast to the rural home, the urban family's roots are not very deep. Also, it tends to get its norms or standards more from the community where it happens to be at a particular time than from long-established traditions regarding the home. Since the communities where the family resides may vary widely in their generally accepted practices, the family and members of the family may become perplexed and frustrated.

There are many other phases of contemporary American culture that could wisely be considered, but let us mention only one. This one is so pervasive and so complex that all we can do is indicate a few of the ways it is affecting our traditional concepts concerning the family. We refer to the expanding of the welfare state. Formerly the two main functions the state performed, at least in our country, were the maintenance of law and order and the protection of the freedom or liberty of its citizens. Possibly inevitably, but at least actually, those functions have been tremendously expanded. Among other things, the modern state—increasingly totalitarian—proposes to watch over the welfare of all citizens from the cradle to the grave.

This, along with urbanization and other factors, has weakened the self-reliance and the inner cohesiveness of the typical American family. There is no longer the strong sense of responsibility for the members of the family that was accepted as traditional in previous generations. This is even true regarding the immediate members of the family, such as children and aged parents. Dawson goes so far as to say that "the very existence of the family as a social unit is threatened by the all-pervasive influence of the state and the secular mass culture."[10]

Dawson may be rather extreme in his statement but there can be no doubt about the effect of the expanding state, with the general atmosphere that it has created, on the American family. The change in the traditional perspective concerning family responsibility affects the work of many of our church and denominational institutions. For example, our children's homes can no longer properly be called orphanages, since the vast majority of those cared for in them are not orphans. Many parents seemingly do not have the sense of responsibility that we have traditionally considered to be theirs. Furthermore, in an earlier day most of the children in these homes would have been provided for by other relatives if one or both parents were dead or could not or would not provide for their children.

Parenthetically, through the remaining part of this chapter, I shall at times be rather specifically evaluative or judgmental. It seems entirely in order for me to state my opinion about some of the changes that have taken place in our traditional family concepts or norms. Some changes have been for the good. Others have unfortunate consequences for the individuals involved, the family, and society in general. Some of the changes have contributed to the weakness and instability of the contemporary American home.

Any change which violates and negates any specifically stated purpose of God for the home is unwise and basically wrong. God created man and woman and established the home, therefore, He knows what is best for them and it. His requirements for the home, as for His individual children, are not arbitrary. They are in harmony with our best interest and the best interest of our homes.

For example, it is my judgment that the shifting to such a large degree of the responsibility for needy parents from the children to any institution or agency, public or private, violates the plan and purpose of God and is not best for the parents or for the children. It is recognized that conditions are different today and that there are cases where the children cannot and should not provide for their dependent parents in their homes. We should not forget, however, that Jesus regarded failure to provide for one's parents a violation of the command to honor father and mother (Mark 7:9-13). Paul plainly says that children or grandchildren should care for a widowed mother or grandmother. He even says: "If anyone does not provide for his relatives, and especially for his own family, he has disowned the faith and is worse than an unbeliever" (1 Tim. 5:3-8).

THE AMERICAN FAMILY: PAST AND PRESENT

What are some additional changes in our traditional American home? There are too many of these for us to discuss them fully and adequately. Some we shall simply mention while others will be briefly discussed. However, before we set forth or evaluate these additional changes, let us examine more specifically the various aspects of the traditional concepts of marriage and the home. Some of these have been more firmly fixed as a part of our traditional family pattern than others. Also, some are far more significant than others.

The following represents the major traditional concepts of the immediate past: Dating began in the middle or late teens. Steady dating, in the main, was postponed until a relatively short time before a couple could normally expect to be married. The initiative regarding dating, proposal of marriage, and physical expressions of affection were male prerogatives. Physical expressions of affection before marriage were to be kept under proper control and were to be expressed only in private. Any full expression of sex other than the physical union of husband and wife was condemned: this was true of premarital intercourse and also sex perversion such as homosexuality. The purpose of the home was to give a legitimate channel for the expression of the sex urge, to provide intimate understanding and fellowship between husband and wife, and to assure the propagation of the race.

Additional traditional concepts regarding the home are as follows: The number of children could be limited, but there was to be no open discussion or advocacy of birth control, particularly the use of contraceptives. Children in the home were to be taught to obey: the discipline of children was considered normal and natural. A childless couple was pitied; they were to accept their childlessness as an act of God—their only hope was in the adoption of one or more children, usually those of relatives. The children in the home picked up their knowledge of sex wherever they could: parents were not considered particularly responsible in this area. Actually the whole idea of sex was considered more or less evil.

It was the man's responsibility to make the living for the family. He was also to be recognized, at least theoretically, as the head of the house and the authoritative figure in the family. Once married, a couple were to stay together except under the most serious provocation—usually sexual unfaithfulness. The so-called innocent party in such a divorce was free to marry again, but not to do so might be a sign of greater moral strength and spiritual maturity. Any case of unusual need by a member of the family, such as a crippled, deformed, or mentally retarded child or an aged or needy parent, grandparent, or even aunt or uncle, was to be cared for in the home. In the case of the death of a husband or wife, the surviving mate was free to marry again, but he should wait at least a year and not be in too big a hurry about looking around. You may think of other traditional concepts concerning marriage and the home, but an adequate examination of what has happened to these would certainly involve considerable time.

What seem to be the developing concepts that have challenged or are in the process of challenging, if not actually displacing, many of the traditional ideals for the home in American culture? Let us adapt what Commanger[11] said in his definitive book of several years ago. The old taboos and the old integrities are dissolving. Puritanism is giving way to hedonism, inhibitions to experimentation, and repression to self-expression. Advertisers pander shamelessly to the erotic instinct, motion pictures and television appeal to it, novelists exploit it, and all use a franker vocabulary than was formerly customary or permitted. What has been the effect of all this on our traditional concepts of marriage and the home?

There has been an artificial and premature stimulation of the sexual development of immature youngsters. The tendency has been to date and to go steady at an earlier age. There has been much sexual experimentation involving many young people in premarital sexual intercourse and others in homosexual practices. And some of these young people are active in the life and work of our churches. The greater ease with which contraceptives, including "the pill," may be secured not only at the drug store and the department store, but at the filling station, is a factor in the prevalence of sexual irregularities.

The childless couple not only can secure children for adoption but there is now held out to them the hope or the temptation, depending on the perspective, of artificial insemination. The status of women is changing in the home and in society. It is uncertain whether her so-called emancipation has been a blessing or a curse to her, her family, and society in general.

The tendency is to remove the father as the symbol of authority in the contemporary urbanized American home. Gibson Winter has pointed this up in a particularly effective way. He says that "the family world is a woman's world, where 'mom' rules and dad visits." He further says that however big the father may be "on the job, at home he has to fit into a going concern as a minor shareholder."[12] He suggests that in the American home "we are allergic to authority, but we cannot escape it."[13] By removing the father as an authority symbol, a vacuum has been created. Vacuums have a way, however, of being filled. This one is filled by the mother who should be the affectional, love, or tender symbol in the home, or it is filled in many homes by the children themselves. Winter, quoting "Whom the Lord loveth, he chasteneth," correctly suggests that "the license that leads to the rule of children is an unloving way of exercising responsibility."[14] Children need discipline. They need the loving but authoritative symbol of the father in the home.

There has also been some rethinking and revising of traditional views regarding divorce and remarriage after divorce. Many factors have contributed to a more lenient position regarding divorce and remarriage inside and outside the church. An increasing number of pastors and other counselors are no longer legalistic in their approach to the problems of the divorced. They are more considerate than formerly of the people that are involved. They tend to treat each case as a distinct case. This, in the main, is an improvement over former days, but we should not forget that we are to do what we can to preserve the home and to work out the problems of husbands and wives within the framework of the home. We are to point them to the resources of the Christian faith. The grace and goodness of God will enable many of them to make a livable or workable adjustment, even to the lack of adjustment.

Furthermore, as those who work from a Christian perspective, we stand under the constant challenge of the purposes of God for the home. His original purpose and his intentional will is one man and one woman joined together as husband and wife for life. We cannot escape the words of Jesus: "What therefore God has joined together, let no man put asunder," and again as He says, "from the beginning it was not so. And I say to you: . . ." (Matt. 19:6, 8-9).

With medical advances that make it possible for doctors to prolong the lives of the incurably ill, it is more or less natural that euthanasia should be discussed more and more. There may not be any serious questions, in definitely terminal cases, about the use of negative euthanasia, where the doctor simply does not utilize all the drugs and techniques that are now available to keep a person alive. Positive euthanasia, where there is an artificial speeding up of death or the taking of life, is another matter. It is difficult to believe that this will ever be approved by any culture that retains even a semblance of Christian values.

Let us conclude by saying that the home is very responsive to the culture, but that the Christian home has a point of reference outside of the culture. Just as the Christian church should place some limits on its adjustment to the culture, so should the Christian home. Furthermore, the Christian church should help to strengthen and stabilize the Christian home so that both the church and the home might be more effective witnesses for God in and to the world.

Part III

RACIAL PROBLEMS

Race and race relations continues to be one of the major problems in many areas of the world. Some astute students of world affairs consider it the number one problem of the contemporary world. It is a social and political problem but also a moral and religious problem, if one can wisely separate the latter from the former.

In Part III as in Part II we shall begin with a biblically based chapter and conclude with one on the impact of our culture. In between these chapters are a biblically centered chapter and one that touches on some of the most perplexing aspects of the contemporary racial situation in the United States.

Chapter 9

BIBLICAL TEACHINGS AND RACE RELATIONS

The Bible in various ways has been brought into the contemporary racial controversy. It has been used to defend every conceivable position, although there is little material in the Bible directly related to race relations.

This is not to say, however, that there is nothing of significance in the Bible on race. There is an abundance of teachings and concepts that are relevant to the racial situation. To deny them and their relevance to contemporary life would be to deny the Gospel itself. In this chapter we shall attempt to set out briefly a few of the basic biblical concepts that may properly be applied to the race problem.

THE NATURE OF GOD

The proper beginning for a study of the teachings of the Bible on race relations, or on any other issue, is in its teachings concerning God. He is the point of reference in the Christian religion. He is the source of authority in Christian theology and in Christian ethics. For example, in the latter the final determinant of right and wrong is in the will of God. That will is revealed, however, not only by what God says and does, but also and basically by what He is. His will is grounded in His nature. If we want to know God's will for us in the area of race relations, let us begin with a study of the nature of God as it is revealed in the Bible.

The first thing that impresses us about the God of the Bible is that He is a Person. He has all the qualities essential to personality: the power to think, to judge, to feel, to will, to communicate. We discover that He is not only a Person but that He is a moral Person. He is a God of holiness, righteousness, and justice.

The fact that God is a moral Person has significant implications for us in our relations to Him and to our fellowman. While we should be faithful to the formal requirements of our religion, this faithfulness will not make us acceptable to God if we have left undone the weightier matters (see Matt. 23:23). Those weightier matters have to do with our relations to our fellowman.

God, who is holy, righteous, just, and merciful, expects His children to possess these same qualities. His word to the people of Israel was, "You shall be holy; for I the Lord your God am holy" (Lev. 19:2). What is true of holiness is true of every other moral quality that God possesses. This fact has tremendous significance for race relations. God expects us to manifest His spirit, His attitude toward all men of all races. God cannot be the ruler of all unless He is sovereign over all. He cannot be limited in His interest or activity to one or two restricted segments of life. The God who created the heavens and the earth is concerned about everything in the heavens and on the earth. This means, among other things, that God has a will concerning every area of human relations, including race relations.

This sovereign God of the universe, who is creatively active in the life of the world and who exercises dynamic control over the world, is revealed in the Bible as Father. The idea of God as Father is found in the Old Testament (see Deut. 32:6; Isa. 63:16; 64:8; Jer. 3:19), but it is particularly prevalent in the life and ministry of Jesus. He gave to the idea new depth and meaning. "He enriched it beyond recognition."[1]

Jesus referred to God as "the Father," "my Father," "your Father," and in the model prayer as "our Father." All of these usages are of importance to the Christian, but "our Father" is particularly significant for us in the study of race relations.

When we pray, "Our Father," we should remember that every other man and woman, boy and girl in the world, regardless of class or color, who has been brought into union with God through faith in Christ, can likewise pray, "Our Father." Are we broad enough, big enough, Christian enough to include them within the circle of our prayer? This may not be much of a problem if they are on some mission field, but what if they live down the street, across the tracks, or in shantytown? What if their skins are red, yellow, or black: can we still pray with them, "Our Father"? If we cannot, then we have failed to catch the spirit of our Father and their Father; we are not acting like members of the family of God.

THE NATURE OF MAN

The biblical conception of man has major significance in the realm of race relations. This has been implied previously.

What does the Bible reveal concerning the nature of man? We shall not attempt to set out the entire biblical doctrine or estimate of man. We shall limit ourselves to a few ideas that are most pertinent to our discussion.

The Bible clearly reveals that all peoples are from one family stock. Back of every race of men is the human race, which gives unity to all. This concept of the unity of the human race is basic in the Old Testament. This is true whether one goes back to the creation story for the beginning of human life or to the story of Noah and his family as the source of the races of mankind.

Paul, in his sermon on Mars Hill, set out pointedly the idea of the oneness of the human family. He said that God "made from one every nation of men to live on all the face of the earth" (Acts 17:26). There are different interpretations of the meaning of the two words, "from one," some interpreting "One" to refer to

God, while others—the majority of commentators—make it refer to one source or family. Williams and Phillips both translate the expression, "from one forefather."

Regardless of which idea is correct, Paul stressed the oneness of God and the unity of mankind. What a long way we would go in solving our problems in the area of race relations if we accepted men and women as members of the human family rather than members of a particular race, class, or caste!

Add to the preceding the fact that all Christians are in the spiritual family of God, have been redeemed by the blood of Christ, and have been brought into union with Him, and we lay the foundation for the solution of all problems of human relations. How can any child of God, when he considers all of these things, justify or defend his prejudice and discrimination against any man because of his class or color?

Another concept in the biblical view of man of major importance for us is the fact that man was created in the image of God. Varied meanings are given to "the image." Central to any correct interpretation must be the idea of personality. God is a person, man is created a person. A person can think, judge, feel, and will, all of which involve freedom of choice. Possibly no one quality is more basic to personality, however, than the capacity and the necessity for communication.

Whatever may be the correct interpretation of the "image of God" in man, there is no question concerning the importance of the image for human relations in general and for race relations in particular. The image of God in man gives to man his worth and dignity. God Himself, on at least one occasion, related directly the high value He placed on man with the fact that the latter was created in His image (Gen. 9:6).

The important thing for us to remember is that *all* men are created in the image of God and that Christ died for all to restore that image, which had been marred by sin. This means that all should be treated with respect. No man who has been created in the image of God, no man for whom Christ died should ever be treated as a mere means or instrument but always as an end of infinite value. This should be just as true of the Negro yardman, or elevator operator, as it is of one's husband or wife, one's son or daughter. One is created in the image of God just as much as the other.

Another idea concerning the nature of man, which is quite relevant to the present racial problem, is the Christian position, maintained rather consistently, concerning human equality. The Christian conception of equality is closely related to the idea of the image of God in man. Really, the only sound basis for human equality is the fact that all men have been created by God and that all have been created in the image of God. This means that men "are equal to one another in all that is involved in being a man."[2] They are equal in being although not in performance, equal in essence although unequal in capacity. Furthermore, they are all equally dependent upon God.

The idea of equality is particularly important within the family of God. The only difference God recognizes in men is in their relation to Him. Those who have come into the family of God through union with Christ are equally children of God and can be assured that they are equally precious in the sight of God. This idea of the equality of all who have come into union with Christ is a central theme in the epistles of Paul (see 1 Corinthians 12:12-20; Galatians 3:26-28; Ephesians 2:13-16; Colossians 3:11).

If all of us had a proper understanding of our relation to God as creator and ruler, we would see how foolish and irrelevant is the whole discussion of the supposed innate superiority and inferiority of races. In the presence of God, the creator and sustainer of all, there is no room either for haughty egotism or for a cringing sense of inferiority and defeat. This is particularly true of those who have come into the family of God through union with Christ. They are children of the King. There is no partiality in His family.

THE WORK OF CHRIST

The fact that Christ died for all men, along with the fact that they were created in the image of God, makes man of more worth than all things material. In other words, man's value is derivative: "It lies in *relatedness to God*." And, we should not have to remind ourselves that Christ died for one man as much as another. He knows no class or color line. His abiding invitation is, "Whosoever will may come." The only condition for coming is faith, and the way of faith is open to all.

Also, Christ "has broken down the dividing wall of hostility" ["the barrier that kept us apart," Williams] (Eph. 2:14), not only between the Jew and the Gentile but between all other groups that have let a wall or a barrier divide them. This He has done and will do by making us one, or "one body" in Him. When we become "one new man in place of the two" (Eph. 2:15), there is unity instead of diversity and peace not only with God but also with one another.

The secret of peace with one another is our peace with God. By reconciling both Jew and Gentile to God, by bringing them into one body, which was accomplished through the cross, Christ brought hostility to an end (Eph. 2:16). This hostility could mean hostility to the law, but it might mean that he "has put a stop to the hostility between us" (Williams). Whether or not the latter is a correct translation, it is a correct idea. We do need to remember, however, that what has been accomplished by Christ becomes a reality in human society only as we cooperate with Him. If we will let Him, He will make us one, He will remove the hostility that divides us into warring class and racial camps. "Race and national distinctions vanish in Christ."[3] And let us not forget that He is our only hope. He and He alone will bring peace with God and with our fellowman. All human animosities will disappear as we are made one in Him, who is the Prince of Peace.

A similar emphasis is found in that wonderful passage on the resurrected life in the Colossian letter (Col. 3:1-17). Paul tells the Colossians to put off the old nature and then admonishes them to put on the new nature, or new self. He states that this new nature is being renewed, or "is in the process of being made new" (Williams). Phillips translates the expression as follows: "The new man is out to learn what he ought to be." The renewal, in one sense, is a process. When we are brought into union with Christ, we unfortunately bring into that experience many of the weaknesses and limitations of the old self. We need to maintain a constant process of education or of renewal "in knowledge." This knowledge, if it is to be most significant for us, must not be simply theoretical. It must become a living experience, a vital phase of our lives. It is doubtful if we really learn anything until we have expressed and verified it in life.

The end or goal of the Christian's knowledge, which is being constantly renewed, is the full realization or restoration of the image of the Creator. There is a sense, of course, in which the image is restored when we become children of God, when we are brought into union with Christ, who is the exact reproduction of the original image. But what child of God would dare to say that the original image has been completely restored in him? As we grow in our likeness to the One who gave his life to restore the image in us, we will grow in our likeness to the One who originally created us in His image. It was Paul who said that we "are being changed into his likeness from one degree of glory to another" (2 Cor. 3:18). The rapidity of the change depends on our cooperation with Him. He will mold us more and more into His image or likeness, if we will let Him.

Some conscientious Christians fail to see the relevance of all of this to human relations. Paul, in the passage in Colossians, makes the relation very specific. He says, "Here ["In this new relation," Williams; "In this new man," Phillips] there cannot be Greek and Jew, circumcised and uncircumcised, barbarian, Scythian, slave, free man, but Christ is all, and in all" (Col. 3:11). Notice how strong and positive the statement is. In this new relation, which results from the new nature, man-made differences "cannot be," "there is no room for" them. Even the Scythians, the most barbaric of the barbarians, are included. In Christ the most radical human differences are erased. Hostile camps that divide men are abolished. If Paul were writing today to your church or mine, do you suppose he would say, "Here, or in this new relation, there cannot be Negro and white?"

Let us refer back to Paul's emphasis on our progressive renewal in knowledge, which certainly means our progressive attainment of the image of God. By combining verses 10 and 11, and emphasizing maturing and the elimination in Christ of man-made divisions, it would mean that Paul suggests that the Christian's ethical and spiritual maturity, his likeness to the image of God can be measured by the degree that cultural, national, and racial differences have no significance for him. Does this suggestion tend to make us a little uncomfortable? Are we still babes in Christ in our racial attitudes? Spiritual maturity on the part of God's people of all races would go a long way toward finding a solution for our present problems.

Will we not admit that the ideals that Paul sets out, not only in these verses from Ephesians and Colossians but elsewhere, are still a long way ahead of most of us as Christians? We would insist, however, that "race distinctions . . . disappear in Christ and in the new man in Christ," and that He "has obliterated the words barbarian, master, slave, all of them, and has substituted the word *adelphos* (brother)."[4] Our task is to appropriate what he has already accomplished.

GOD'S ATTITUDE TOWARD MAN

There are many things in the Bible concerning God's attitude toward man, but of particular significance from the viewpoint of race relations is the fact that God's love, to use Luther's expression, is "round and whole," that He shows no partiality or is no respecter of persons. There is abundant evidence of this fact in both the Old Testament and in the New Testament.

For example, Jesus, over and over again, revealed that He was no respecter of persons, that He showed no partiality. He was a friend of the despised publicans and sinners (Matt. 11:19), ate with them (Luke 5:29-30), and chose one of them (Levi or Matthew) as a member of the inner circle of disciples. The Master, on at least one occasion, had some kind words even for a harlot (Luke 7:36-50). He was friendly in His attitude toward and relation to the Samaritans, with whom the Jews had no dealings. He introduced the Samaritan woman to the living water (John 4:1-42), did not even bother to reply to the charge of the Jews that he was a Samaritan (John 8:48), possibly considering the charge of no consequence. Jesus made a Samaritan the hero of one of His greatest stories (Luke 10:25-37), called attention to the fact that of the ten lepers who were healed only the Samaritan in the group returned to thank him (Luke 17:11-19), and included Samaria, in a special way, in the commission given to His disciples (Acts 1:8). One cannot imagine Jesus giving any consideration to the outer conditions of men or the color of their skin. He looked on the heart.

There is abundant evidence in the Scriptures that the followers of Christ recognized the importance of the "no-respecter-of-persons" principle. In general, it permeates the entire New Testament. We find it emphasized specifically in the writings of Peter (1 Peter 1:17) and Paul, who made it the theme of the first chapters of Romans. The latter stated the principle specifically (Gal. 2:6) and implied it in many places. An example of this is in his wonderful statement in Galatians 3:28 (compare Rom. 10:12; 1 Cor. 12:13; Col. 3:11), which Williams translates as follows: "There is no room for ["Gone is the distinction between," Phillips] Jew or Greek, no room for slave or freeman, no room for male or female, for you are all one through union with Christ Jesus." Notice the words, "there is no room," which is a simple statement of fact. "The point is that 'in Christ Jesus' race or national distinctions . . . do not exist, class differences . . . vanish, sex rivalry . . . disappears."[5] Robertson correctly says that this is a radical statement and that "candour compels one to confess that this goal has not yet been fully attained."

If Christians do not begin to comprehend more fully what it means to be impartial and to apply this great truth more consistently, "it is possible that future historians may declare the irony of ironies—that in the middle of the twentieth century, fight promoters and baseball managers did more for emancipating the Negro than did the churchmen."[6] Let all of us as Christians seek to eliminate from our lives all prejudice and all discrimination against any class or race. Our heavenly Father is no respecter of persons, He shows no partiality; may we increasingly be like Him.

MAN'S RELATION TO HIS FELLOWMAN

The Bible, in the main, contains a twofold message: how men who are lost can be saved, and how saved men are to live. There is found a twofold emphasis regarding the latter: how the saved man is to live in relation to God (the vertical), and how he is to live in relation to his fellowman and to the society of men (the horizontal). There is no question in the Bible about which of these relations comes first. Where they are found together, right relation to God is first. There is a sense in which right relation to one's fellowman derives from his right relation to God. The Bible does reveal, however, that right relations to man inevitably result from one's right relation to God, and hence being right with one's fellowman is a proof that one is right with God.

One illustration of this close relationship is found in the teachings of the New Testament concerning love. When Jesus was asked for *the* great or chief commandment, He said that it was supreme love for God. Although He was not asked for a second, He thought it wise or necessary to add, "And a second is like it, You shall love your neighbor as yourself" (see Matt. 22:34-40). These two go together. The second is like to the first, not only because it is a commandment of love, but it is also like it in importance. Together, the two fulfill all the requirements of God as found in the law and the prophets (cf. Rom. 13:8-10; Gal. 5:13-14; James 2:8).

The close relation of love for God and one's fellowman is particularly central in 1 John. The theme for the first portion of this little book, which is so rich in its insights into the Christian life, is that *God is light*, and the theme for the last part is that *God is love*. The one who knows God, who has been brought into union with Him, has love abiding within Him. It is natural then that "He who does not love does not know God; for God is love" (1 John 4:8).

Let us repeat that our heavenly Father expects us to be like Him. He is love; we show our kinship to Him by loving one another. He is impartial; we are to be no respecter of persons. He manifests the fatherly attitude toward all, even those who are not in his spiritual family; we are to show the brotherly spirit toward all, even those who are not our brothers in Christ. Are we honestly striving to be like our heavenly Father? Do we see the relation of all of this to the contemporary racial situation?

Chapter 10

THE WORD OF GOD AND THE RACES OF MANKIND

Soper, in his relatively old but still standard book on racism, says that the word "race" was used for the first time to designate different human groups in 1749.[1] The term is used with various meanings in contemporary literature. There are books on the races of a particular geographic area, such as Africa.[2] There is rather general agreement, however, that there are three major divisions or families of races.

The designation by different authors of these divisions varies considerably. For example, a group of experts formulating a statement for Unesco made the following threefold division: the Mongoloid, the Negroid, and the Caucasoid.[3] Kephart classifies the major divisions as black (Indafrican), yellow-red (Turanian), and brown-white (Aryan).[4] With slight variations, other scholars suggest that the major divisions are black or Negroid, yellow-brown, and white. There are many distinctive ethnic groups within these major divisions.

Characteristics other than color are frequently used as a basis for the classification of the races. Some of these characteristics are language, eye color and form, texture of hair, shape of nose, cheek bones, or head, and body structure in general. However, the most convenient classification for our purpose is on the basis of color. After all, our main concern is not with the races of mankind but with what we find in the Word of God concerning those races. When we accept color as a basis for the major racial divisions, we should remember that the colors blend into one another. It has been suggested that if all living human beings were arranged in a single sequence according to color resemblance, there would be no sharp breaks in the line. The difference from one individual to another would be almost, if not entirely, imperceptible.

In this discussion, we shall emphasize, in the main, two things: what is revealed in the Scriptures (1) concerning the origin of the races, and (2) concerning the relation of the races. There will be a concluding section in which we shall set forth in broad outline a Christian approach to human relations based on the biblical revelation.

THE ORIGIN OF THE RACES

The Bible reveals, as suggested previously, that all men have come from one common stock. It was Paul at Mars Hill who said, "And he made from one every nation of men to live on all the face of the earth, having determined allotted periods and the boundaries of their habitation" (Acts 17:26). Whether the "one" in this statement refers to God or to one forefather, Paul's sermon stressed the oneness and sovereignty of God and the unity of mankind. Montagu says that this statement by Paul "is in perfect accord with the findings of science."[5] As the Unesco report says, "Scientists have reached general agreement in recognizing that mankind is one: that all men belong to the same species, *Homo sapiens.*" In other words, all men of all races belong to one great over-arching race: the human race. Their similarities are more striking and significant than their dissimilarities. The oneness of mankind in the creative work of God is far more important than the racial distinctions so sharply drawn in many areas of the world.

The Word of God also reveals that man was created in the image of God (Gen. 1:26-27; cf. 5:1-2). This was and is true of all men of all races. This is the basis for the high value placed on man in the Bible (see Gen. 9:5-7). The image of God concept has tremendous significance not only for race relations but also for human relations in general. For example, in Genesis 2:18, it is recorded that the Lord God said, "It is not good that the man should be alone; I will make him a helper fit for him," or as the American Standard Version says in its original reading, "answering to" Him.

Why was it not good for man to be alone? One answer is that he was created with a biological nature that could find its fulfillment only in one who would answer to or supplement him. In other words, it is not good for him physically to be alone. There is, however, another sense in which it is not good for him to be alone. This involves something that is deeper and more significant than his physical need. This deeper need stems from the fact that man was created in the image of God, that he was created a person. This means, among other things, that he was created for fellowship or communication. Such fellowship is necessary if he is to find his fulfillment as a person. On the highest level, this fellowship is with God, but man also requires fellowship with fellow human beings. The most meaningful aspect of this fellowship is in the intimate relation of husband and wife.

It possibly can properly be inserted here that any attitude or activity that mars the image of God in man or disturbs, destroys, or makes difficult man's fellowship with God and his fellowman is sin. In other words, sin separates man from God and man. The healing love of God unites.

Let us return to the main line of our discussion. If all races are derived from one common source, how can we explain the wide variations of the races of mankind? We are not concerned here, except in a very secondary way, with the scientific explanations. That is the task of the scientist, particularly the anthropologist. Our concern is with what we find in the Bible that might explain the origin of the various races. It is encouraging to discover that the findings of many scientists support, at least to a degree, what we find in the Scriptures regarding the races of mankind, although the Bible does not claim to be a book of science. The purpose is redemptive.

We previously quoted Montagu, a prominent anthropologist. Another anthropologist, Kephart, after setting forth his conception of the various racial divisions, says, "It is interesting to observe how well Biblical accounts confirm the foregoing outlines of racial relationships."[6] The author is referring here primarily to Genesis 10:1-32 (cf. 1 Chron. 1:1-27), where at least some of the sons and grandsons of Shem, Ham, and Japeth are listed. He suggests that the races known at that time (about 2300 B.C.) were "(1) sons of Shem (Turanian semities), (2) sons of Ham (Aryan Hamites), and (3) sons of Japheth (Aryans of the North)."

The line of Ham is of particular interest to us because so much emphasis has been given to it in racial controversies, past and present. It is quite interesting from our perspective to know that many anthropologists agree that the Hamites were Aryan and in a broad sense belonged to the white or white-brown racial division. This is true of anthropologists such as Kephart and Seligman. The latter, in his study of the racial divisions of Africa, distinguishes between what he calls the Eastern Hamites and the Northern Hamites. He suggests that the Eastern Hamites roughly correspond to Ethiopia and the Northern Hamites to Mizraim or Egypt, but that the latter also include the contemporary North African nations whose boundaries do not coincide "with any geographical or racial division."[7] Seligman has several other chapters on distinctive racial groups in Africa including one on the "Bantu," and another on "The True Negro," who is not of the Hamitic line. He makes the following statement concerning the relation of the Hamites to the Negroes. "Almost everywhere in this vast area the Negro carries in his veins a greater or less proportion of Hamitic blood and has been influenced by Hamitic culture."[8]

An interesting aspect of any study of the Hamitic line would involve some consideration of the curse of Canaan. We do not believe, however, that a thorough examination and evaluation of the curse (Gen. 9:25) is necessary in connection with this study. A personal conclusion is that there is no sound exegetical or scientific basis for applying this curse to the Negro. The children of Canaan were not black and, so far as is known, they did not reside or move into Africa. They were in Palestine when the Israelites conquered the Land of Promise. As previously suggested, some of the other descendants of Ham did go to Africa, but the curse was not upon them. Furthermore, while these other children of Ham may have been dark-skinned, it is rather generally agreed that they were not black or Negroid. We would agree with Ryle that the application of the curse on Canaan "to the African races is an error of interpretation."[9]

There is one other incident in the Old Testament that is sometimes cited as an explanation for different races. It is the confusion of tongues at the Tower of Babel. This incident may help to explain the scattering abroad or the distribution of the races, but it does not explain their source. It seemingly purports only to explain differences in languages.

What can we correctly conclude from the biblical record concerning the origin of the various races? One thing is their common source. Whether we go back to Noah or to Adam, the races of mankind came from one human stock, and back of that is the creative act of God. We also find in the record of Noah and his sons and their descendants a suggested source for at least most of the major divisions and some of the subdivisions of the races of mankind. However, the Bible does not trace in detail the migrations of the descendants of Shem, Ham, and Japheth. Some hints or leads can be derived from the names of certain descendants of Noah, such as the sons of Ham: Cush or Ethiopia, Mizraim or Egypt, and Canaan. We also get some insight from the tribes descended from certain individuals. For example, Canaan became the father or the ancestor of the Jebusites, who controlled Jerusalem until the days of David (2 Sam. 5:6-9). He also was the father of the Amorites, the Girgashites, the Hivites, and others (Gen. 10:15-18; cf. Ex. 3:8, 17; 23:23; 33:2). There are some other hints that are at times somewhat tantalizing. For example, it is said of the sons of Javan, who was a son of Japheth: "From these the coastland peoples spread" (Gen. 10:5). Similarly, it is said that "the families of the Canaanites spread abroad." Nimrod, a son of Cush of the line of Ham, "went into Assyria, and built Nineveh" (Gen. 10:11).

In spite of these hints or suggestions, we must depend, in the main, on the anthropologists for information about the relation of existing racial groups to the great family lines descended from the sons of Noah.

RELATION OF RACES

Let us turn now to the other major aspect of our discussion: the Word of God and the relation of the races of mankind. In the Old Testament, the emphasis generally was on the separation of the Israelites from the peoples around them. It should be mentioned that those immediately around the Israelites were not of another color. They were from the white or the white-brown racial division, the same as the children of Israel.

The comparison of the Israelites and their neighbors, from the racial perspective, would be somewhat comparable to comparing an Englishman with an Italian or a Turk. It would not be comparable at all to the relation of white and Negro people.

It is also clearly revealed that the emphasis on separation was primarily, if not exclusively, religiously motivated. God had made a covenant with His people; they were not to "make a covenant with the inhabitants of the land" (Ex. 34:10-12)—the Amorites, Canaanites, Hittites, Perizzites, Hivites, and the Jebusites. Rather, they should tear down and destroy their symbols of worship: their altars and their pillars. The Israelites were not to worship any God except the Lord. To do so was to play the harlot. Also, if they entered into covenant with the inhabitants of the land, their sons and daughters would intermarry, which would be playing the harlot with their gods (see Ex. 34:13-16).

There are similar exhortations in Deuteronomy (7:1-5), with seven nations or peoples mentioned, and in Ezra (9:1-2), where eight nations or peoples are named. An examination of each of these references will reveal that the specifically stated motivation was religious. For example, in Deuteronomy it says, "You shall not make marriages with them, giving your daughters to their sons or taking their daughters for your sons." Now notice the reason: "For they would turn away your sons from following me, to serve other gods" (Deut. 7:3-4). Ezra admonished the people of Israel to separate themselves from the peoples of the land "with their abominations." He says that through marriage "the holy race" had been mixed with the peoples about them (Ezra 9:1-2). Ezra in talking with God, says, "shall we break thy commandments again and intermarry with the peoples who practice these abominations?" (9:14). For Ezra, the marriage of foreign wives meant the breaking of faith with God (10:2).

These prohibitions or exhortations against intermarriage in the Old Testament might be used to argue against the marriage of a Christian and a non-Christian, or conceivably against the marriage of those of different national stocks, but they cannot correctly be used to support arguments against racial intermarriage.

Really, an objective study will reveal that no specific teachings of the Bible can be used properly to support any particular position on intermarriage. In contrast to the Scriptures cited against intermarriage, references can be made to the actual marriage of some of the outstanding personalities of the Old Testament to those of other peoples, including some prohibited by the law and by Ezra. Abraham (Gen. 16:3) and Joseph (Gen. 41:50) married Egyptians, descendants of Mizraim, one of the sons of Ham. Moses married a Cushite (Num. 12:1), and Cush was one of the sons of Ham, and his descendants are frequently referred to in the Scriptures as Ethiopians (see Ps. 68:31; Isa. 18:1). David was a son of Ruth of Moab, one of the groups with whom Ezra had forbidden the Jews to marry. The greatest descendant of the Davidic line was Jesus; the blood of the nations flowed in His veins.

The preceding has not been presented to defend intermarriage. There are valid common-sense arguments against certain interracial marriages in our culture. We have set forth this biblical material because in the present racial controversy the Scriptures have been so abused and misused. Let us all, regardless of our viewpoint regarding our racial problems, seek, as best we can, rightly to divide or handle the word of truth (2 Tim. 2:15).

When we move from the Old Testament to the New Testament, we find that the Jews, in the main, continued the rather strict view of the Old Testament concerning their relations to other peoples. We see this in their relation to Gentiles in general but to the Samaritans in particular, who were a mixed race or group. It was the Samaritan woman at the well who said to Jesus that the Jews had no dealings with the Samaritans. But a new dimension, at least new in compassion, concern, and outreach, had entered the scene. Jesus came to reveal the nature of God and His attitude toward and His will for man. He did not let such man-made divisions keep Him from revealing the Father's love and concern for peoples of all classes and cultures. He not only revealed to the Samaritan woman that He was the Living Water, but He tarried for a while to minister among her people. No wonder the first revival outside of Jerusalem was in Samaria (Acts 8:4-8).

The disciples of Jesus were slow to learn the lesson of their Master. It took a vision on a housetop to convince prejudiced Peter that he was not to call common or unclean what God had cleansed (Acts 10:15). Through the leadership of the Divine Spirit, he was led to interpret correctly this vision. It was in the house of Cornelius that he said that God revealed to him that he was not to call any man common or unclean (Acts 10:28). No wonder that the first words of his sermon in the house of Cornelius were, "Truly I perceive," or "I see quite plainly," (Moffatt) or "I am catching on"[10] that God is no respecter of persons or shows no partiality (Acts 10:34).

Paul saw clearly that when we become new creatures in Christ Jesus the distinctions between racial and cultural groups are erased, and in this new relationship "there cannot be Greek and Jew, circumcision and uncircumcision, barbarian, Scythian, slave, freeman." Why? Because "Christ is all and in all" (Col. 3:11); the oneness is in Christ. In Him racial, cultural, and national distinctions may not disappear, but they become of no consequence. It is Christ who breaks down the dividing wall of hostility, or "the barrier that kept apart" (Williams) Jew and Gentile in the temple area and elsewhere (Eph. 2:14). Would not Paul say the same thing concerning any class, cultural, or color barrier that separates God's children in our day?

In Christ, in the deepest sense, there is neither Jew nor Gentile, slave nor free, male nor female. Why is this true? Because we "are all one in Christ Jesus" (Gal. 3:28; cf. 1 Cor. 12:13; Eph. 6:8). The God who made us one in the beginning wants to make us one again in Christ.

CONCLUSION

Let us briefly consider some guidelines for Christians in the area of human relations—guidelines that stem directly from the nature of our biblically revealed faith.

When one becomes a child of God, he is brought into a life-changing union with Christ. This is a union so vital that Jesus compared it to the vine and the branches. The branches are an integral part of the vine; the life-blood of the vine flows through the branches and is the source of their fruitfulness.

The one who is in union with Christ inevitably gets something of His perspective concerning sinning, suffering humanity. He sees his fellowman through the eyes of God, and since the God whom Jesus revealed was no respecter of persons, the child of God should not be.

Through our union with Christ, we are brought into the family of God, into the fellowship, the community, the *koinonia* of the redeemed. Those within the fellowship have a common heavenly Father and hence they are brothers and sisters in Christ. The contemporary fellowship, as was true of the Jerusalem church, should be "of one heart and soul" (Acts 4:32). This oneness should go so far and be so deep that those within the fellowship would willingly share with one another in times of need. Furthermore, this fellowship should be inclusive of all of God's redeemed children.

There should be a special love for those within the fellowship. The one commandment that Jesus gave to His disciples was that they love one another. If we love God, the parent, we should love one another who are His children. John, in his typically plain way, says, "If anyone says, 'I love God,' and hates his brother he is a liar" (1 John 4:20), and "brother" is determined by relation to our common Father and not by color or culture. Love is "the best way of all" (1 Cor. 12:31, NEB) within this fellowship. It never fails or never ends (1 Cor. 13:8). For that and other reasons, those of us who are within the fellowship should make love our aim or "put love first" (1 Cor. 14:1).

This love, however, that stems from God who is love is not and cannot be restricted to the Christian fellowship. Jesus, in the Sermon on the Mount, pointedly said that it should reach out even to our enemies (Matt. 5:43-44). The last two rungs of Peter's ladder of Christian virtues (2 Peter 1:5-7) are "brotherly affection," or "brotherly love" *(philadelphia)*, and love *(agape)*. But notice that love in general, or *agape*, is the top rung of the ladder. Love within the Christian fellowship is of such a nature that it inevitably will spill over. Those within that fellowship do not live isolated lives; they live in the world. The life they live within the *koinonia* naturally finds expression in and through their lives where they live, work, and play. They go as representatives of the fellowship, or, better, wherever they are, there is the church of Christ—the fellowship of the redeemed.

Some may say that this is idealistic. True. Our Christian faith is idealistic, but this does not make it irrelevant. Let those of us who approach the human situation, race or otherwise, from the Christian perspective remember that ours is a distinctive contribution. Let us not become so involved in the political approaches to the problems—approaches that are valid and valuable—that we fail to magnify and to be channels for the love of God. And we need to be sure that we ourselves are so solidly grounded in that love that we can and will continue to love when our love is rebuffed or rejected. This should be true if the rebuff or the rejection comes from within our own racial group, or even our own Christian group, as well as from those of other races, cultures, and convictions. How tragic it would be if, in the struggle for the rights of all—rights that are legitimate and should be provided—we should lose our respect and love for one another as individual persons, actual or potential children of God.

Chapter 11

LAW, ORDER, AND MORALITY

It may be assumed that the word "law" refers primarily to human law—the laws of towns, cities, counties, states and the nation. However, there are various classifications of laws, such as Thomas Aquinas' threefold division of natural law, human law, and divine law. The natural law and the divine law[1] when properly understood have considerable significance for human relations. This is true, although some Protestant theologians have little if any place in their thought for the natural law.

A discussion of the natural law and the divine law, along with other concepts of the law, might be of considerable interest. However, we will restrict our discussion, in the main, to the human law. While some portions of this study may seem to be rather theoretical, it is hoped that its relevance throughout to the contemporary racial situation will be apparent.

After setting forth some "Background Convictions" or underlying principles, we shall consider the relation of "Law and Morality," followed by a discussion of "Law, Order, and Justice." In the latter section. we shall give major attention to the relative importance of order and justice, particularly in a time of revolution and change. This will be followed by a consideration of "Love, Justice, and the Law."

BACKGROUND CONVICTIONS

There are a number of convictions that provide the background for the remainder of this chapter.

1. Our world is in the midst of the most serious crisis or revolution it has known since the days of the Renaissance and Reformation. The stirring among the underprivileged in the South and throughout our nation cannot be understood apart from this revolution which is characterized by a restless movement of the masses of the world. This movement, in turn, is both a result of and an important factor in the crisis or revolution.

2. The expanding welfare state, with its totalitarian trends even in countries with a democratic tradition, seems to be an inevitable expression and product of the contemporary age. Such a state, with its New Deal, Fair Deal, and the Great Society, is inevitably concerned for the welfare of all the people. In other words, an expanding state more or less naturally has an expanding concern.

3. The law cannot remain static. It must be living and dynamic, particularly if it is to meet the needs of a changing society. It cannot remain static in its formulation, its interpretation, or its application. This means, among other things, that legislators and judges on local, state, and national levels should not only be thoroughly acquainted with history, they also need to be well grounded in sociology, psychology, and other social sciences. Such sciences have a proper place in the formulation and interpretation of the law, including the Constitution of the United States.

4. Democratic institutions and the democratic way of life cannot be preserved without a respect for law and for those who make, interpret, and enforce the laws. Extremists at both ends of the present racial struggle have contributed, in the contemporary period, to a rather prevalent contempt for law and for public officials in general.

5. The individual person is of supreme worth or value in our American way of life and in the way of the West. This means

that laws and institutions exist primarily as instruments to serve the individual and not as ends to be served by him. This is a basic difference in the way of the West and communism, and political totalitarianism in general.

6. Although men are unequal in many ways, they are equal in all that makes them men. They stand equal before God and are to be treated as equals by the law. Their equality and inequality have been compared to triangles. Triangles may be made of different materials or may be of many different shapes, but there are certain common characteristics of all triangles. These common characteristics are three sides with the combined length of any two sides longer than the third side and with the three inner angles totaling one hundred and eighty degrees.

7. The individual person finds his fulfillment in a community of persons. There is no person without other persons.

8. Rights and responsibilities belong both to the individual person and to the community of persons. These two—rights and responsibilities—must be kept in proper balance for a healthy individual person and for a healthy community of persons, whether family, neighborhood, city, or state.

9. Because of the preceding, the law, along with those who interpret it and enforce it, should seek to protect and promote the well-being of the individual person but at the same time seek to promote the common good. These two go together. The individual person is served when the common good is promoted, and the good of society is dependent upon the well-being of individual persons.

We shall return to and expand one or two of these background convictions while the others will not be referred to again.

LAW AND MORALITY

Law and morality, in a sense and to a degree, belong together. An understanding of their close relation along with their distinctive approaches and emphases has considerable significance for an accurate appraisal of the contemporary racial situation.

Supreme Court Justice Oliver Wendell Holmes, Jr., a few years before his appointment to the Court, made the following statement: "The law is a witness and external deposit of our moral life." He further said that the history of the law "is the history of the moral development of the race." The same could be said concerning the law of our nation: in its formulation and interpretation it has been—and is—the history of the moral development of our people. Justice Holmes also said that "the law is full of phraseology drawn from morals, and by mere force of language continually invites us to pass from one domain to the other without perceiving it."[2] Although law and morality are distinct, as we shall point out shortly, they do impinge on one another, if they do not actually have a considerable overlap.

One's viewpoint concerning the relation of law and morality will be determined to some degree by his perspective concerning the nature of the state. Particularly important is whether one considers the state a natural and good institution (Aristotle, Aquinas, the Roman Catholic Church), or an institution necessitated and permeated by sin—the position of Augustine and most Protestant theologians of the past. The more one is oriented toward the thought of Aquinas, the more closely he will relate human law and the divine law, and also the more closely he will relate law and morality.

Law and morality may be merely different "manifestations of the same thing,"[3] but at least there are noticeable differences. For example, they have in common a sense of responsibility, but they differ in the motive appealed to and the sanctions or punishment imposed for violation. In the area of law the punishment is primarily physical—loss of property, of liberty, and as the last resort, loss of life. The punishment is imposed from without. "The law is not normally concerned with interior attitudes but with external conduct."[4] In contrast, in the realm of morality the appeal and the punishment is primarily inner. Also, in the area of morality, the moral value of actions is determined primarily, although not exclusively, by the motives of the actor.

Furthermore, acts to be moral must be voluntary; they must be free from outer compulsion. This freedom of man as a moral person to respond responsibly and not through compulsion, as Tillich says, is man's "greatness but also his danger."[5] Tillich also suggests that "a moral act is not an act in obedience to an external law, human or divine. It is the inner law of our true being, of our essential or created nature, which demands that we actualize what follows from it."[6] Some of us would have preferred for Tillich to have left out the reference to the divine law. After all, the divine law is in harmony with and an expression of our essential nature.

The same author also says that "the moral imperative is the demand to become actually what one is essentially and therefore potentially." He defines the moral act as one "in which an individual self establishes itself as a person."[7] I believe we may properly go beyond what Tillich says and say also that the moral act is one in which one assists another individual self to become a person.

An additional difference between law and morality is in content or scope. Law is concerned almost exclusively with those standards of behavior that are considered essential for the existence of the community. It is really minimal in its requirements. Morality has no such limits. It calls for conformity to an ideal. It is concerned with standards or patterns of conduct that are considered good or right. Really, morality implies a dualism—right or wrong, good and evil. This dualism, in turn, indicates, as Berdyaev says, "that man is a wounded creature,"[8] and that distinguishing between good and evil is a painful process for him.

One reason for this painful process is the tension between what is and what ought to be. This tension is seen not only within morality, but it is also seen within the law and between the law and morality. For example, the idea of what is good for the individual and for society changes from generation to generation. This is even true when one moves over into the area of the theoretical aspects of the Christian ethic. Whether the norms change or not, man's comprehension of those norms is never complete or final. If the latter is correct in the more theoretical area, it is just as true in the applied or practical areas. Actually, morality, and particularly the Christian ethic, is not fulfilling its mission unless it creates some tension between what is and what ought to be. And let it be repeated over and over again that there is no progress toward the ideal in our individual lives or in our society without tension.

The developmental idea of necessity is and must be prominent in both law and morality. It was Justice Holmes who said that "the law embodies the story of a nation's development," while Roscoe Pound's frequently quoted statement is: "Law must be stable and yet it cannot stand still." Pound also said that in the legal area we must make room for what he calls "the received ideals of the time and place." One function of the courts is to help to keep the law abreast of the times. Just as my theology professor used to say that every generation needs to rewrite its theology, so every generation needs to rewrite, or at least to reinterpret and reapply, its laws. If the law lags too far behind the needs of the people, pressure will build up which will result in ignoring the law or possibly even rebellion against it.

Perhaps it can be safely stated that there is no real progress in law or morality except for some creative souls who will set their faces toward the fuller light of the approaching tomorrows, while at the same time they respect the past and the present. These prophetic spirits have on occasions found themselves out of step with their times. They are creators of tension and frequently find themselves torn between their love for their people and for things as they are and what they interpret to be the word and will of God for them.

These creative persons are at times the martyrs of one generation and the heroes of the next. Let us never forget, however, that the true prophet is one who speaks for God to and on the behalf of his people, and particularly on the behalf of the underprivileged. He does not seek more for himself but more for others.

LAW, ORDER, AND JUSTICE

Carl Friedrich suggests that "in the philosophical speculations concerning law and right, law has recurrently been presented or oriented *either* toward justice *or* toward order." The tendency is for the orientation to be toward order in quiet and ordinary times. Friedrich further says that "the situation changes in times of great revolutionary upheavals and cultural crises."[9] The orientation in such times is more toward justice. The contemporary period is such a time of crisis, with society, in the United States and elsewhere, changing at an unprecedented pace.

While it is more or less natural that the emphasis in the contemporary period should be on the use of the law to attain justice, law and order should not be neglected. After all, Paul admonished the Roman Christians to be "subject to the governing authorities" because those authorities are from God, and one "who resists the authorities resists what God has appointed" (Rom. 13:1-2).

It should be remembered that methods may be used in an effort to attain justice that tend to undermine respect for the law and for those who administer the law. While we do not condemn all marches and demonstrations, we do suggest that the courts and other orderly processes should be first used to the fullest. If no redress of grievances can be secured in that way, then we cannot rule out other methods of protest. Care should be exercised, however, that respect for law and for public officials in general is maintained. Any disobedience of the law should be done regretfully and without encouragement to rebellion. Particular care should be exercised in large group demonstrations. Such a group may become a mob composed of people who have no clear conception of what justice is and little idea about the purpose of their protest.

On the other hand, it is tragic in a time of revolution for the privileged and the powerful to use the cry "law and order" to defeat or attempt to defeat the purposes of justice. While some extremists in the civil rights movement have tended to undermine the authority of police and others who enforce the law, segregationists and the radical right movement in general have contributed to an undermining of respect for law, for the courts, and for government in general. In other words, many of those who cry the loudest for "law and order" have contributed to the breakdown of respect for law, at least as interpreted by the courts and enforced by the federal government. What they are doing results in disorder rather than order.

The major question is where the primary emphasis should be: on order or justice? In a period of rapid change and revolution, it is quite evident that justice should be given primacy. The Christian worker, including the Christian missionary, faces at times a perplexing problem at this point. It is difficult for him to divorce himself from his privileged position and throw his weight on the side of justice for the underprivileged, which incidentally has been the customary stance of the prophet of God. It is difficult for him to distinguish between some of the methods the underprivileged may use to attain their goals, which he may disapprove, and the goals they are seeking, which he should approve. If the privileged deny the legitimacy of the grievances of the underprivileged, they play into the hands of the communists or at least those who seek to provide the leadership for the underprivileged. If we want to preserve our way of life, or what is more important, if we want to be on the side of justice and right, we had better seek to catch step, at least to some degree, with the restless movement of the masses in our midst. Let us never forget, however, that while we should be on the side of justice, we should not neglect order.

It will help if we will keep in mind Friedrich's conclusion that justice and order are dependent on one another. He says, "They cannot be realized in a legal community except jointly."[10] Let us repeat, however, that one may be faced with a choice of priorities and that in a revolutionary age the priority must be with justice.

LOVE, JUSTICE, AND THE LAW

In the area of human relations in general and race relations in particular, there is a dimension more comprehensive than justice because it is inclusive of justice. That dimension is love or, possibly better, *agape*, a word that many scholars believe should not have been translated but simply brought over intact into modern languages. At least *agape* represents a distinctive quality or type of love. It is a love that gives itself unselfishly to the object loved: "For God so loved the world that he gave his only Son" (John 3:16a); "Christ loved the church and gave himself up for her" (Eph. 5:25b); "Greater love has no man than this, that a man lay down his life for his friends" (John 15:13).

God *is agape*. Wherever *agape* is found in human life and relations, God is its source. It is potentially the most distinctive contribution of the Christian movement to the community of men. The deeper needs of individual persons and of the community of persons cannot be met apart from *agape*. Unfortunately, in the above statement we felt it necessary to use the word "potentially." How tragic that so few Christians and Christian groups have been and are effective channels for the love or *agape* of God.

It should not be necessary to insist that no attempt should ever be made to substitute love for justice. This is a matter, however, that disturbs some people. A keen young Negro Ph.D., in a discussion period following an address, asked the searching and pointed question: "Is there not a danger that Christians will tend to substitute love for justice and make love an empty sentimentality?" A good answer to the question is found in the following statement by Tillich: "Love, in the sense of *agape* contains justice in itself as its unconditional element and as its weapon against its own sentimentalization."[11] In a rather typical paradoxical statement, Reinhold Niebuhr says that "love is both the fulfillment and the negation of all achievements of justice in history."[12] For Tillich, love is the creative element in justice.[13] The unconditional demand for justice is "in the very nature of *agape*" and "if love takes justice into itself justice is not diminished but enhanced."[14]

Niebuhr contends that equal justice in society is an attainable goal but that absolute love in society is not. Whether this position is true or not does not in any way affect the validity of love as the ultimate ideal in the Christian life. Niebuhr himself would agree that *agape* is abidingly relevant at least in the sense that it is the ultimate ideal and stands in judgment against our imperfect achievement even of equal justice.

The law cannot produce love. The latter stands above and beyond law, although there is a relatively close relationship between the two. Love comes to fulfill the law, not to destroy it: "The second mile of love presupposes the first mile of law."

One distinctive quality of love is what Tillich calls the drive toward unity, "the reunion of the estranged."[15] This estrangement may be between God and man or between man and man. The only sound hope for a reunion of the estranged in the area of race relations, at least in our culture, is the love of God in the hearts of his people.

The law can provide for justice. The courts can break down the physical walls that separate. For example, the authority of the government can be used to achieve desegregation, but it cannot achieve meaningful integration.

There is no real integration, which should be the ultimate goal in human relations, without a removal of separating barriers in the minds and the souls of men. The only hope for the elimination of these barriers or walls is in Christ. This is expressed graphically in the Ephesian letter. Phillips' translation is as follows:

> But now, through the blood of Christ, you who were once outside the pale [Gentiles] are with us inside the circle of God's love in Christ

Jesus. For Christ is our living peace. He has made a unity of the conflicting elements of Jew and gentile by breaking down the barrier which lay between us. By his sacrifice he removed the hostility of the Law, with all its commandments and rules, and made in himself out of the two, Jew and Gentile, one new man, thus producing peace. For he reconciled both to God by the sacrifice of one body on the cross, and by this act made utterly irrelevant the antagonism between them. Then he came and told both you who were far from God and us who were near that the war was over. And it is through him that both of us now can approach the Father in the one Spirit (Eph. 2:13-18).

Would it not be wonderful if all our people could see that in Christ "the antagonism" between us is irrelevant? How wonderful if we could realize that the war is over.

The original plan was to close this chapter with several conclusions similar to the background convictions that were stated in the beginning. I believe it to be the part of wisdom, however, for each of us to draw our own conclusions as individual Christians and also for the churches with which we are affiliated. Surely we will agree that it is time for our churches to face up to the full demands of the Gospel we preach in this whole area of race.

It may be wise to remind ourselves that the God we worship and serve so imperfectly is the sovereign God of the universe. We can be assured that He has a will for every area of life, including race relations, and that His will ultimately will be done. There will be a time when "the kingdom of the world has become the kingdom of our Lord and of his Christ, and He shall reign forever and ever" (Rev. 11:15).

Chapter 12

CONTEMPORARY CULTURE AND SOCIETY'S RACIAL DILEMMAS

"Society" in the subject for this discussion will be considered as including the institutions of society such as the state, or nation, and the church.

The dictionary definition of "dilemma," which is not entirely satisfactory for our purpose, is as follows: "A situation involving a choice between equally unsatisfactory alternatives." For many of us the choice in the area of race is not between "equally unsatisfactory alternatives." Webster's *Dictionary of Synonyms* gives us some help regarding the word "dilemma." Suggested synonyms are "predicament," "quandary," "plight," "scrape," "fix," and "pickle." Each one of these could be applied in a sense and to a degree to the present racial situation, but the most descriptive one for most of us is "quandary." The latter carries the idea of puzzlement or perplexity.

This quandary or dilemma is a product of our culture. It stems to some degree from the fact that there are idealistic concepts or ideas in the culture that are negated by our present racial pattern. There are also conflicts within the culture. Cultures are seldom, if ever, completely unified. Most of them contain dilemmas that are not fully resolved.

Conflicts within cultures stem, to a degree, from the fact that a culture is composed and, in a sense, is a product of subcultures. One example of such a subculture is a regional or an area culture, such as the Southern region of the United States. A regional or subculture, in turn, may have its own subcultures, ultimately breaking down to distinctive cultures in villages, towns, neighborhoods, and communities. Regional cultures with their subcultures are bearers of the more extensive national culture, but they may contain elements contradictory to some aspects of that culture. For example, the plantation pattern of life with its emphasis on the "apartness" of the races, still maintained as a nostalgic dream by many Southern white people, violates some of the central concepts of our American way of life. And loyalty to the so-called American way of life is professed as loudly in the Southern region as anywhere else in the nation. This creates an inner conflict of soul in many Southerners, which is one reason for the intensity of the dilemma in the South. It also helps to explain the strength and the frequently vitriolic expressions of opposition to the changed status of the Negro. Like the preacher who beats the pulpit, many people are revealing their own anxieties and sins and are evidently seeking to convince themselves of the rightness of their position.

This does not mean that the racial dilemma is exclusively or even peculiarly a problem of the Southern region. It is very definitely a national and even an international problem with the problem in some areas such as South Africa as acute as anywhere in the world. We have simply suggested that a regional culture, which may face serious dilemmas within itself, may also be an important factor in creating the racial dilemma of our American society. To a considerable degree, however, the racial dilemma, which is basically a dilemma between dream and reality or fulfillment, is characteristic of every region of our nation. The dilemma or quandary is experienced by the typical American, and in a special way by sensitive American Christians.

THE NEGRO'S DILEMMA

The dilemma is increasingly acute not only for the white man but also for the Negro and the Negro community. Every step of progress that the American Negro has made has increased his awareness of the deep racial dilemma in our culture. He has become better acquainted with the American dream or creed. He has also become increasingly conscious that the dream or creed has not been applied consistently to him.

Also, for the first time, American Negroes have trained men and women to provide the leadership they need to voice their dissatisfaction. Some of these better trained Negroes themselves face distinctive dilemmas. How far shall they go in identifying themselves with and getting involved in the troubles of their people? Many of them have more in common culturally with middle and upper class white people than they do with the rank and file of their own people. One thing that helps some of them to identify with their people is the fact that they do not have access, in the main, to certain aspects of the white man's culture. The prosperous Negro business or professional man may have climbed the economic ladder, but he finds himself on the lower rungs of the social ladder except among the Negroes.

It is also true that some of the better trained Negroes have a stake in the continuation of a segregated society. This is particularly true, to varying degrees, of lawyers, doctors, dentists, teachers, and preachers. Nevertheless, enough of these professional men and women have become involved in the struggle of their people to provide much of the leadership for contemporary protest movements. One reason why so much leadership for the Negro protest has come from professional rather than business men is the fact that they are relatively free, particularly the ministers, from reprisals by the white community. Support for themselves and their families comes largely from the Negro community. This is less true for the teacher than for other major professional groups among the Negroes.

Negro leaders in the contemporary racial struggle face some

additional dilemmas. Where shall they place their major emphasis: on public facilities, education, politics, or social gains in general? How can they lead the masses of the Negro people to be willing to pay the price for the liberties that are rightfully theirs? Or, should they expect the people to pay the price that some will have to pay? What are the most effective strategies they can use? How far and how fast should they seek to move? Can they press so fast and vigorously that they will alienate some of their white friends? Can they win what they are after without the assistance of these white friends? Shall they march or not march? If they organize and lead a march, what should be its purpose? Once public protests, such as marches, are started, can they be controlled? Once the marches have seemingly attained all they can, what is the next move?

There are many other dilemmas that the Negro leader faces, but there is at least one of major proportions: is he primarily to speak for or to the Negro culture? He may be in as much danger as the white leader of becoming a captive of the culture. Is it possible for him to maintain his personal identity and integrity and yet not lose his ability to provide constructive leadership for his people?

The preceding discussion correctly implies that there is a distinguishable Negro culture, which is a subculture of our total American culture. It is unfortunate for the Negro leader and for the Negro culture itself if he becomes a slave of and a defender *in toto* of that culture. Prophetic voices are needed among both Negro and white ministers and laymen.

THE NATION'S DILEMMA

All of us, Negro and white, are involved in the racial dilemma of our society. It represents one of the most complex and pressing problems of our nation. The Supreme Court decision of 1954 and the civil rights laws since that time did not create and, on the other hand, have not removed the racial dilemma of our society. In some ways that dilemma has been more sharply drawn than formerly. It may be that the horn of the dilemma that ultimately must be chosen is seen more clearly, but its choosing is just as painful as ever for many people. Myrdal, ten years before the Supreme Court decision, in the introduction to his definitive study of the racial situation in the United States, said the following:

> The "American Dilemma," referred to in the title of this book, is the ever-raging conflict between, on the one hand, the valuations preserved on the general plane which we shall call the "American Creed," where the American thinks, talks, and acts under the influence of high national and Christian precepts, and, on the other hand, the valuations on specific planes of individual and group living.[1]

In another place he said that "the subordinate position of Negroes is perhaps the most glaring conflict in the American conscience and the greatest unsolved task for American democracy."[2]

The subordinate position of the Negro became a disturber of the conscience of the American and a conscious dilemma for him only when he realized the discrepancy between the American creed or dream and its very imperfect application to the Negro. One essential element in that dream is the democratic faith in and insistence upon the equality of all men. This aspect of our democratic dream has come under considerable attack in recent years. It is being insisted by some that all men are not created equal. Whether or not they are depends on what is meant by equality. They are not created equal in ability. As Sheed says, "There is not a single quality in which all men are equal." He further says that "all men are equal only in the sense that all men are equally men," but that "men are equal to one another in all that is involved in being a man."[3] Sheed also says that "in the Christian view, being a man is so vast a thing, that the natural inequalities from one man to the next are a trifle by comparison."[4]

What is it that makes being a man so "vast a thing"? It is the fact that he is created in the image of God, and that Christ died to restore that image in him. Also, through union with

Christ, man comes into the spiritual family of God and becomes a brother to all who are in that family. These and countless other blessings are available to men regardless of class or color.

Those who stress the inequalities of men should remember that although there may be and are inferior and superior individuals, these inferior and superior individuals are not limited to any one race. Even if it could be proved that there are inferior races, a democracy, if true to its basic concepts, would insist that all citizens of all races are equal before the law, are to have an equal right to participate in their own government, and are to enjoy an equal opportunity for self-improvement and advancement. The racial dilemma in our society, as Myrdal suggests, stems from the gap between our dream or creed and the very imperfect fulfillment of that dream.

It may be, as some people insist, that the gap is natural and even inevitable, but it should not be defended. Some gap between dream and reality does seem to be more or less natural because of the nature of human institutions. Any organizational expression of a great ideal or philosophy always fails to measure up fully to the ideal. Existing democracies fall short of the democratic dream. They do not express consistently the basic concepts that gave them birth. The results of this failure are not too unfortunate as long as the dream remains alive. The dream cannot be kept alive indefinitely, however, if there are premeditated and deliberate violations of it, and particularly if those violations are defended as in harmony with the dream.

This is a factor in the dilemma of our nation. Our people generally know now, even if they did not formerly, that the members of minority groups are treated as second-rate citizens. They know that the basic concepts of our democratic way of life are not applied fully and consistently to Negroes and other minority peoples. How long can we retain our faith in the American dream or creed when such inequalities are so clearly evident in our nation, and are defended by so many of our people?

The racial situation also creates a dilemma for our nation in its relation to other peoples and nations. The world is in a crisis period with the masses everywhere on the move. These restless moving masses, many of whom are colored, tend to identify themselves with the struggle of the American Negro. We and our allies of the West are competing with the communists for the leadership of those masses. Whoever provides that leadership will largely determine the future of the world. Possibly the most serious handicap we have as we seek to win the restless masses is our failure to apply our democratic principles to the Negroes in our midst.

THE CHURCH'S DILEMMA

The contemporary racial situation not only creates some dilemmas for our nation but also for our churches. One reason for this is the church's contribution to and involvement in the democratic dream. Some of the most central concepts of that dream, such as the dignity and worth of the individual, are derived primarily from the Christian movement. While we do not equate democracy and Christianity, we do believe that the church has a considerable stake in the preservation of the democratic dream or creed.

The church's dilemma is also a result of its divine-human nature. The dilemma is not merely something outside of the church; it is within the church. As a human institution, it cannot avoid the impact of the culture, while as a divine institution, it cannot escape its responsibility to speak for God to the culture. There is no realm in which the contemporary church feels more keenly the tension created by its twofold nature than in the area of race.

It seems that our churches have a "rendezvous with destiny." The future of the Christian cause in America and around the world may be determined to a considerable degree by what our churches do in the days immediately ahead about the racial dilemma or dilemmas of our communities, our nation, and our churches. "If we do not attempt honestly to apply the Christian spirit and Christian principles to race relations, how can we expect others to respect our Christian claims or to hear and accept the message we proclaim?"[5]

What are some of the central concepts of that message, concepts that are strikingly and tragically relevant to the contemporary racial situation? Let us state a few of the more significant ones, most of which have been discussed previously. They are as follows: Men of all classes and races come from the same family stock; they belong to the human race. God created man in His own image, and in His relation to and dealings with men He shows no partiality or is no respecter of persons. He is the sovereign God of the universe, which means, among other things, that He is concerned with and has a will for every area of life, including the relation of races. Christ died for all men that through faith in Him they might be raised from death to walk in newness of life. The individual person is worth more than all things material. Jesus plainly taught that men cannot be right with God unless they are right with their fellowmen. They are not only to love God supremely, they are also to love their neighbor as themselves, and their neighbor is anyone in need.

These ideas or principles are enough to underscore the revolutionary nature of our Christian faith and to point up the discrepancies between what our churches preach, what we as individual Christians profess to believe, and what we and our churches practice.

Another aspect of the message the church proclaims is the New Testament teachings concerning the church itself. Many Protestants pride themselves on being a people of the Book. They claim that where it speaks, it is authoritative. This means that our churches have an unusual responsibility to be New Testament churches. Such being the case, what are some of the chief characteristics of a New Testament church?

Paul, in an expression found only in his epistles, refers a

number of times to "the church of God" and in one place to
"the church of the living God" (1 Tim. 3:15). He also speaks of
"the churches of God" (1 Thess. 2:14, 1 Cor. 11:16). He addresses the Corinthian Christians as "the church of God which
is at Corinth" (1 Cor. 1:2). This succinctly suggests or sets forth
the divine-human nature of the church. It is at Corinth, but it is
the church of God. It is not Peter's, Paul's, or Apollos' church;
it is God's church.

The New Testament also clearly reveals that the church is the
body of Christ—an emphasis that is particularly prevalent in First
Corinthians and Ephesians. As Christ's body, it is to do His
work in the world. It is an instrument to be used for His glory.
He is its head. It is to get its instructions from Him.

What would it mean in the area of race if churches took
seriously the fact that they are "churches of God," that they
are "the body of Christ?" Many of our churches will not
welcome, and some will not even admit, a Negro as a visitor in
a regular service. Some of our churches may have unique problems because of their constituency and their church polity, but
how can any church justify the exclusion of the Negro? How
can we as members of the churches explain this to ourselves?
How can we explain it to Negro Christians? What is more
disturbing—how can we explain it to our Lord, who is the head
of the church?

Since the church is the church of God, He should say who
comes into the fellowship of His church. Since the church is
the body of Christ, it seems that He, as the head of the church
rather than a prejudiced minority or even a prejudiced majority,
should have a right to decide who comes in the door of the
church and sits in the sanctuary that has been dedicated to Him.
"How terrible for any group that calls itself a church to tack a
sign, literally or figuratively, across the front door to its building
saying, 'for white people only' or, 'No Negroes admitted'! God
does not have any such limiting signs for entrance into his
family. God's church should not have any such signs, and it

would seem that it cannot and will not have if it is really his church."[6]

The church is also a fellowship, a community, or a *koinonia* of the redeemed. Within that fellowship there should be no respect of persons or partiality. James pointedly says, "My brethren, do not hold your faith in our glorious Lord Jesus Christ, with an *attitude* of personal favoritism" (James 2:1, NASB). One translation of the verse is as follows: "Do not you, who call yourselves believers in Christ, disgrace your faith by exhibitions of partiality."[7] Phillips' translation is as follows: "Don't ever attempt, my brothers, to combine snobbery with faith in our glorious Lord Jesus Christ." Are we snobbish? Do we and our churches disgrace the faith with "exhibitions of partiality"?

Some of our churches and many of their members are increasingly embarrassed by the segregation pattern of those churches. It has been called "the scandal of the churches." "How tragic it would be if the churches became the 'last bulwark of racial segregation'! What a paradox if secularism and secular institutions 'outchristianize Christianity'!"[8]

THE CHRISTIAN'S DILEMMA

This chapter would not be complete without a brief statement concerning the individual Christian's dilemma. As a citizen, he is involved in the dilemma of the nation. As a church member, he is deeply involved in the dilemma of his church. If he is serious about applying Christian principles to everyday relationships, he is frequently in a quandary—perplexed if not frustrated. What can he do constructively about the deep-seated racial dilemma in our society?

The conscientious Christian faces over and over again the whole matter of the best Christian strategy. Is it wisest and best for him to seek to apply fully the Christian ideal now or to move gradually toward that ideal? If he does not apply it fully now is he failing to do so because he is honestly convinced that such represents the most effective strategy, or is it because he is a moral coward, afraid to face the consequences of full application? These are questions that more or less constantly disturb the socially and morally sensitive Christian; the more sensitive he is, the more he is under constant tension."

This tension, which is a product of the dilemmas Christians face in the area of race as well as in other areas, is particularly acute for the pastor and others in church related vocations. Many of them are under constant pressure, a pressure that comes not only from without but also from within their own souls as they face up to the truth of the Gospel they preach and teach. Those of us who are in this group may consider it wise at times to keep silent about our racial situation. It may be that we would lose the opportunity to minister, at least to a particular church or group, if we spoke all that is in our hearts concerning the racial dilemma that plagues us, our churches, and our society. It is possible, of course, that our heavenly Father would have us run that risk. Each individual must answer to God for himself. This much I am sure about: if we do not speak because we are afraid, then we are unworthy to be called servants of God and particularly to be known as prophets of God.

There are some other people who face unusual dilemmas because of our racial dilemma. These are our missionary friends, more than half of whom serve among the colored peoples of the world, and most of the others serve where there is a mixture of population without any segregation. Let us permit the missionaries to speak for themselves. May we let their words search our hearts and challenge us and our churches.

A. Luther Copeland, a former missionary in the Orient and now professor of missions at Southeastern Baptist Theological Seminary, says, "The missionary movement carries about its neck the mighty millstone of our inconsistency as it operates in the colored world, and it staggers more and more beneath this weight."

John E. Mills, formerly of Nigeria but now working in the Gold Coast of Africa, states the dilemma as follows: "We must quickly come to the place where we treat all men on the basis of their individual worth, or else we must pull down our missionary banners and leave the carrying out of the Gospel to others who will do so."

Glen Morris of Thailand searchingly says, "It is conceivable to people that some 'bad' people may discriminate against colored people, but it is utterly inconceivable to them that Christian churches should do so. And we are absolutely at a loss when we attempt to explain it." He further says, "I have no hestitation in saying that race discrimination in America and other countries primarily identified with Christianity is a tremendous factor against us as we try to witness for Christ here these days."

The problem of the missionary has become markedly increased because of the modern means of communication. A veteran missionary in Nigeria says that race riots in his home town in the South were in the newspaper in Nigeria the next morning and that the police dogs in Birmingham were on their TV screens that night.

This same missionary statesman, I. N. Patterson, points up another dilemma of the missionary as follows: "We are in the unenviable position of doing too much along this line (race) to suit many of our people at home, while we do not do enough to suit our friends here who cannot understand how Christian people could practice discrimination, and particularly in the house of God." In an understanding, and yet a prophetically challenging statement, he also says, "We sympathize with our people as they try to adjust to a new era and a new order, but we feel that with our Lord and Savior we must recognize with the prophet that 'My house shall be called a house of prayer for all people.'"

The Christian, in the homeland or on the mission field, is faced with a real dilemma in the area of race. He is a citizen of two worlds. He cannot escape the influence of the mores, but he must answer ultimately to the Master. There is a more or less constant conflict in his soul between the environment, "which would restrain and limit him, and the Christian message, which would lift and challenge him." The tension that is thus created is the main hope for progress in the area of Christian race relations. In turn, "the most reliable assurance of an easing of the tension is a movement toward the Christian ideal coupled with a genuine sense of humility and a continuing spirit of repentance and renewal of fellowship with God, who has 'made from one every nation of men to live on all the face of the earth.' "[10]

Part IV

POLITICAL PROBLEMS

The four chapters of this Part deal with representative problems in the political areas. The first chapter, which is rather general, is followed by two chapters dealing with more specific problems: religious liberty and democracy. The latter attempts to relate the principles of political democracy to democracy in church and denominational structures. It is believed that the last chapter on "This Revolutionary World" is a suitable closing for our study together.

Chapter 13

CHURCH, STATE, AND THE CHRISTIAN ETHIC

The study of church and state may be approached from many different viewpoints. One that is seldom used and yet one that can be rather fruitful is from the perspective of the Christian ethic. There are some aspects of the Christian ethic that are of major significance for the church, for the state, and for their relation to one another. It will be suggested that some phases of the Christian ethic help to determine the origin and nature of these basic institutions, along with the limitations of their authority. Some attention will be given to the relation of both the church and the state to the individual and to his relation and responsibility to them.

SOVEREIGNTY OF GOD

The ultimate point of reference in the Christian ethic is God. What Bruce said some years ago about Old Testament morality could be said of the Christian ethic and of the Christian life in general. He said that Old Testament morality revolved around God "as the planets around the sun."[1] It is, however, the nature of God rather than His existence that is of major importance for the Christian religion and its ethic.

The Christian ethic is ultimately grounded in the nature of

God. His will, which is the source of authority in the Christian ethic, is in harmony with and an expression of His nature. Similarly, His expectations of His children are based upon or are derived from His nature. He expects them to be like Him. "You shall be holy; for I the Lord your God am holy" (Lev. 19:2). So God would say regarding every moral quality that He possesses. He is righteous, just, merciful, loving; He expects His children to possess these qualities. How do we know that God possesses these qualities? We know not so much by statements or pronouncements in the Bible to that effect but by the things that He did and does, by the way He acted or acts. He dealt justly; He was just. He was righteous in His judgments; He was righteous. What was true of Him in the past is true of Him today.

Since God is a moral person, He expects not only His children but also governments and other organized social groups to be moral or ethical. He requires these groups to treat people justly. He seems to be particularly concerned about the poor, the underprivileged, the strangers, the neglected. They are His special protégés. Just as is true of the individual, no human collective, including the church or the state, can be right with God, who is a moral person, simply by observing certain ceremonies or by meeting some prescribed formal requirements. Through the prophets God pronounced judgment even upon His chosen people because of their sins, not only directly against Him but also against their fellowmen.

The fact and the nature of God's judgment suggest another truth about Him, revealed in the biblical record, that is significant for the study of church and state. He was and is the judge of the nations. He is no absentee landlord, no disinterested spectator. He was active in the affairs of Israel and her neighbors. His judgment came not only upon Israel and Judah but also upon other nations. Many of these nations thought of their gods as being active in their affairs but not in the affairs of other nations. The latter was a distinctive contribution of the Jewish comprehension of God. Their God, who is our God, is the same yesterday, today, and forevermore. This means, among other things, that He is creatively active in the affairs of contemporary nations as well as being active in and through the churches.

The whole idea of the sovereignty of God is of major importance in any understanding or proper interpretation of church and state. God cannot be the sovereign God of the universe if He is interested and active in only one segment of life. He is not the sovereign God if all He is concerned about is what goes on in the sanctuary on the Lord's Day, as important as that is. No, God is also concerned about what goes on in the home, in the school, on the farm, in the shop, in the legislative hall, and in the judicial chambers. He is creatively active in the totality of life. Anything less than this conception will mean a narrow, distorted idea of the Christian life and ethic.

The world is suffering from a religion which is too limited in its conception of its own significance. It is entirely too satisfied with its prevalent compartmental status. As a result, the trend is to dismiss it "as an adjectival and peripheral concern."[2] Berdyaev says that organized Christianity is "degenerating because it has been relegated to a corner of the human soul and has ceased to be a totalitarian attitude toward life, as, of course, it should be."[3] Berdyaev is not advocating an ecclesiastical totalitarianism but a spiritual totalitarianism. The Christian religion needs to permeate every phase of life with its basic spiritual and moral concepts. Every realm should be brought under the influence, and in a very real sense made to serve, the purposes of God.

This concept means, among other things, that the state or government as such, as well as the church, was founded by God and is to fulfill His purposes. We read, "on this rock I will build my church" (Matt. 16:18), and "Let every person be subject to the governing authorities. For there is no authority except from God, and those that exist have been instituted by God" (Rom. 13:1). Christ's words to Pilate were, "You would have no power over me unless it had been given you from above" (John 19:11). Forell suggests that it is the power or authority of the state that has its origin in God.[4] Whether the state, with its authority, was a part of God's original purpose for man or was a result of and a remedy for sin, it came from God. Rommen states the Roman Catholic position, which is shared by many other Christians, when he says, "So deeply is the state rooted in human nature that it would have grown also in the *status naturae purae*, i.e., without the Fall. The state is not a consequence of sin."[5] In contrast, "Luther not only saw the origin of the state in man's sin, he also found in the state a special embodiment of sin."[6] Similarly, Brunner says, "In the necessity of the State we recognize the consequences of Original Sin."[7]

There is a sense in which both the state and the church are divine-human institutions. It is the divine-human nature of these institutions that creates much of the tension within them and also between them.

The state is divine not only because it was ordained or instituted by God but also because He decrees in general its purposes. The big overall purpose for the state is really the same as it is for the church: to promote the rule, the reign, or the kingdom of God among men. The church and the state are to use different methods in the promotion of the rule or reign of God, but they are both to promote it. The state can legitimately use the earthly sword to approve the good and to restrain and punish the evil (Rom. 13:3-4). The church is restricted to the spiritual sword, to the Word of God.

The state is a divine institution in the sense that God is its ultimate authority. He holds governments as well as strictly religious bodies responsible. They are all stewards of His and are being and will be judged by Him. He judges them, among other things, on the basis of their cooperation with Him. He is creatively active in every area of life. Are they, both state and church, creatively active with Him in achieving His purpose, in advancing His rule, His reign, His kingdom?

DIGNITY OF MAN

The Christian ethic is not only grounded in the nature of God, but also in the nature of man. The latter, as well as the former, has considerable significance for church and state. The thing about the nature of man that is most important from the viewpoint of the Christian ethic is the fact that man was created in the image of God. Brunner suggests that "the whole Christian doctrine of man hangs upon the interpretation of this expression."[8] Whatever the expression "the image of God" may mean—and it has been interpreted from several viewpoints—it certainly includes the idea of personality. God is a person; man is a person. There is no person without other persons. This, in turn, means that man was created for communication or companionship. He has both the capacity and the necessity for such companionship. God said that it was not good for man to be alone, so He created for him "a helper fit for him" or someone to answer to him (see Gen. 2:18, ASV, marg.), someone in whom he could find his fulfillment, someone who would supplement or complement him. However, the deepest need of man, and the area where he finds his highest fulfillment is in communion with God.

Calvin might think of the image as a mirror which reflects God. However, for him it is not a static "but a dynamic reflection by way of active response to the Will of God and to the Word of God."[9] Man's communion with God is really initiated by God Himself. Eichrodt suggests that man alone of God's creatures is confronted and addressed by God as "thou."[10] Augustine's classic statement was, "Thou madest us for Thyself, and our heart is restless, until it repose in Thee." While God takes the initiative in His communication with man, yet communion on the human or the divine level always involves two persons. Man was made for fellowship with God. He is homesick for God. Deep down he knows that he is "seeking some city which has foundation whose builder and maker is God."[11] Brunner suggests that "man, in contrast from all the rest of creation, has not merely been created by God and through God, but in and for God."[12]

Man's creation in the image of God, created "in and for God," gives to him his twofold nature. He is of the natural order and yet, because he is created in the image of God, he stands above nature. "He has the capacity for indeterminate transcendence over the processes and limitations of nature."[13] It is this fact, along with the companion fact that Christ died to restore the image of God in man which had been marred by sin, that gives to man his worth and dignity (see Matt. 16:26).

The inherent rights of man are rooted in or based upon his sovereign worth, which in turn is founded primarily upon the fact that he was created in the image of God, created for fellowship with God. The fundamental rights of man, variously called human, natural, or divine, "belong to man because he is man, and are valid even against society."[14] They are the "Unalienable Rights" of the American Declaration of Independence, and, according to John Locke, the state has the "positive duty of preserving these rights."

Because of his worth and because of the unalienable natural rights that are his, man is to be treated with respect by his fellowman and also by the state and the church. He is never to be used as a mere instrument or tool. Kant expressed something of the innate dignity of man when he said that "we should use humanity whether in our own person or another, always as an end, never as merely a means." But it should never be forgotten that man's value is based upon the fact that he was created in the image of God. Separate him from God and he is worth no more than an animal. Berdyaev says that *"where there is no God there is no man."*[15]

The rights of the individual provide one basis for the control by the people, in so far as such is valid, of both the church and the state. The church and the state, in the main, are to serve man rather than to be served by him. This viewpoint is very basic in the Western way of life.

The individual, on the other hand, should recognize that he not only has some inherent rights but that there also must be some limitations of his rights. Really "there is no freedom without some surrender of freedom."[16] Some limitations of the individual's freedom are necessary for the health both of the individual and society. The Western world has been plagued with an unbalanced individualism. Contemporary culture has sought to raise the idea of individuality beyond the limit set for it in the Christian faith.[17] There has arisen "a pernicious separation of individual rights from individual duties."[18] Such a separation tends to lead to social and moral anarchy. The Christian viewpoint is that there is no right or privilege without a corresponding duty or responsibility. For example, the individual not only has some basic rights that should be protected by the church and the state, but he also has some specific responsibilities to these and other institutions.

It may sound paradoxical, but one of the greatest responsibilities of the individual is to accept the responsibility of freedom. There has been a remarkable and in some ways a perplexing tendency in the contemporary world for men to surrender voluntarily their basic liberties rather than to accept the responsibilities those liberties entail. The leaders of both the church and the state have some responsibility to help to keep alive within man not only the willingness but also the determination to be free. Murray suggests that the "flight from freedom" is not only occurring in political life "but also in philosophy, in social life and in religion."[19]

The individual needs to see, however, that his greatest freedom cannot be found in isolation from others and the group but in fellowship with others in the group or community. Man's nature demands communion with others. "A person cannot exist as a self-contained and self-sufficient Absolute."[20] The communities or institutions of society "are innate in the God-created individual with his capacity and need for completion."[21] The leaders of church and state, however, should never forget that while the individual as a person needs the community and the institutions of the community for his fulfillment, yet he always tends to go beyond them. This dependence upon and yet independence of the church and the state and other institutions stem from the transcendental-earthly nature of man. He is a part of the natural order, but being created in the image of God, he stands apart from and above that order.

The transcendental nature of man is a factor in the limitations of the authority of both the church and the state. The final source of authority not only for the church and the state but also for the individual is God. This is particularly true of the individual who is a Christian. God has reserved for Himself the final word to His child. Conscientious children of God have always said, "We must obey God rather than men" (Acts 5:29), whether those men represented the church or the state. The fact that God speaks authoritatively to the soul or the conscience of His child is one of the chief sources of tension for the Christian. There arises at times a conflict between what he interprets to be the voice of God and the commands of his state or even the standards or expectations of his church. And, it should be remembered that "the will of God is not mediated to the individual by the church or the state."[22] This means that the individual has the right but also the responsibility of determining for himself what the will of God is for his life. Both the church and the state should recognize the final authority of the voice of God for His child. Such a recognition will be best for the church and and the state, as well as for the individual. Without such freedom there would be little chance for new creative moral and spiritual insights and ideas—ideas that mean growth and advancement for both church and state.

Another important element in the Christian doctrine or estimate of man—and one that has considerable significance for church and state—is the fact that he is a sinner. Pascal speaks of the misery and grandeur of man. His grandeur results from his creation in the image of God, his misery results from the sin

that has marred that image. Even the redeemed individual cannot escape entirely the enslavement and the effects of sin. The
fact that man, Christian or non-Christian, is a sinner has serious
consequences for all human institutions. It means, among other
things, that every human institution is tainted or corrupted by
sin. This is certainly true of the state; it is also true of the church.
The latter, as a divine-human institution, is involved in the sin
of the world. The more its human nature dominates, the greater
is its involvement in the sin of the community and culture in
which it finds itself. This means, among other things, that no
human institution, including the church and the state, can ever
be equated with the kingdom of God. The latter, which will be
triumphant over history, can never be properly identified either
with history or the historic process—sacred or secular.

THE CHRISTIAN ETHIC

Some may contend that the discussion so far has been theological rather than ethical. Such a viewpoint reveals a rather narrow, distorted conception of the Christian ethic and of the
Christian life in general. The nature of God and the nature of
man are just as basic for the Christian ethic as for Christian
theology. Really, a proper understanding of the Christian life
based on the biblical revelation would convince one that a
sharp distinction between theology and ethics is arbitrary and
unwise. Such a distinction is not in harmony with Christian experience. The two—theology and ethics—belong together, and
their separation, in most ways, has been quite unfortunate.

In this section we shall discuss some central concepts of the
Christian ethic, concepts that are frequently used to describe
the nature of the ethic itself. There are so many of these ideas
or terms, growing out of the breadth and depth of the Christian
ethic, that only two or three of the more significant and relevant ones will be discussed. The Christian ethic could be properly described as an ethic of perfection, of the will of God, of
love, of the Holy Spirit, and of the cross.[23] These descriptive

terms or labels are rather closely related to one another and to the general nature of the Christian ethic. The present discussion will be limited to a consideration of the first three of these —perfection, will of God, and love—as they relate to the church and state.

Since the Christian ethic is ultimately grounded in the nature of God, it would be expected to be an ethic of perfection. God is perfect; He expects His children to be like Him. Jesus specifically said in the Sermon on the Mount: "You, therefore, must be perfect, as your heavenly Father is perfect" (Matt. 5:48). He also taught his disciples to pray:

> Thy kingdom come,
> Thy will be done,
>   On earth as it is in heaven.
>   (Matt. 6:10)

If the Father's will were done on earth as in heaven, it would mean perfection. But, there remains a very pressing and disturbing question: Is this ideal of perfection relevant for human institutions such as the church and particularly for the state?

Some Christian scholars make a rather sharp distinction between the relevance of the Christian ethic of perfection for the life of the individual Christian and for the social group. Niebuhr goes so far as to say that this distinction "justifies and necessitates political policies which a purely individualistic ethic must always find embarrassing."[24] He also says that "group relations can never be as ethical as those which characterize individual relations,"[25] and he goes so far as to say that "the demand of religious moralists that nations subject themselves to 'the law of Christ' is an unrealistic demand, and the hope that they will do so is a sentimental one."[26]

Although there is much validity to Niebuhr's position, which is shared by many others, this does not relieve the Christian from seeking as best he can to apply the ideals of perfection to the groups to which he belongs as well as to his own life. He is to do the best he can and is to recognize as a compromise or an accommodation anything less than the ideal. He may under certain circumstances feel that he himself must choose the lesser of two evils, or to use a distinction of Weatherhead,[27] he may think that he must follow the circumstantial rather than the intentional will of God.

It should be remembered, however, that the lesser of two evils involves some evil, which means that the evil in the decision is to be kept under the constant judgment of the perfect ideal. The circumstantial will of God is never to be identified with or defended as the intentional will of God. It should always point in the direction of and be evaluated in the light of God's intentional will. It is also true that the church, the state, and other human collectives are measured by and must ultimately come to terms with the intentional will of God. That will, which is a will of perfection, stands in judgment against the very imperfect attainment of that will by both individuals and social groups or collectives.

There is a sense in which human institutions are judged by the ideals that are inherent in those institutions themselves. Murray expresses this concept as follows: "The church itself is conceived as an ideal by which the church as an institution is continually judged."[28] What he says about the church he also says about the state. He asks and answers the question, "Is there also an invisible ideal State regulative of the State on earth?" His answer is yes.[29] The "ideal church" and the "ideal state" from the Christian perspective may be equated with God's ultimate will and purpose for those institutions.

The Christian ethic is not only an ethic of perfection and an ethic of the will of God; it is also an ethic of love. This emphasis is central in the New Testament as a whole and particularly in the teachings of Jesus. Niebuhr contends, however, that the ethics of Jesus, including His ethic of love, are "not immediately applicable to the task of securing justice in a sinful world."[30] Niebuhr's viewpoint is that absolute love is not an attainable goal in society, while equal justice is, and hence Christians should give their time and energy to the achievement of the latter.

Even if the Christian ethic of love were not immediately applicable, would this mean that it was irrelevant? No, it is relevant, at least in the sense that it constantly judges society for its very imperfect expressions of that love and even its imperfect attainment of equal justice. And, it should not be forgotten that equal justice will not and cannot be attained apart from love as the dynamic or drive. William Temple says that "love transcends justice,"[31] and "that only when love is in the heart can justice be established in the world."[32] Niebuhr himself says that love is ethically purer than justice,[33] and in his dialectical or paradoxical way he says that "love is both the fulfillment and the negation of the achievements of justice in history."[34] The two—justice and love—cannot be separated "because they are united in God."[35]

There is another sense in which the Christian ethic of love is relevant. At least most would agree that it is to be applied as far as possible by the individual. However, the individual does not live in a vacuum. He is a member of a family, of a church, of a labor union, of a chamber of commerce, of a particular race, and also a citizen of a state. He is under obligation to be as Christian as possible in all of these and other relations. This means that he is to apply as best he can the Christian ethic with its emphasis on love or *agape*.

Even if the love ethic could not be applied immediately, it would still be normative for the behavior of the individual and also for collectives, which would include the church and the state. The love commandment remains the law of life. The ethic of Jesus is "finally and ultimately normative,"[36] not only for the individual but also for the church, the state, and all human collectives. It establishes the norms or standards for every area and realm of life.

Chapter 14

THE SECULARIST THREAT TO RELIGIOUS LIBERTY

It is not the purpose of this discussion to trace the different aspects of the relation and sometimes the conflict between the sacred and the secular. For example, we shall not discuss the relation of the natural and the supernatural, faith and reason, or the church and culture. Rather, we shall concentrate on the threat to religious liberty from secularism in the world and also in the church.

DEFINITIONS

Before proceeding with the main portion of the discussion, let us suggest some working definitions of "secularist" or "secularism" and "religious liberty." A secularist is "one who rejects every form of religious faith and worship, and undertakes to live accordingly."[1] Secularism has been defined as "the ordering and conducting of life as if God did not exist,"[2] or as "an order of life . . . indifferent to the judgment and grace of God."[3] The secularist does not usually deny the existence of God, he simply ignores Him or relegates Him to an insignificant place in life. Life for the typical secularist revolves around the here-and-now. There is no recognition of a transcendent point of reference.

Religion, for him, is the otherwordly refuge of the individual soul, and particularly of the soul that is frustrated and insecure.

Whether or not secularism is a threat to religious liberty will be determined, to some degree, by what is meant by religious liberty or freedom. It is defined in various ways. The Soviet Union, a secularist regime, claims that it provides for religious freedom but from our perspective it has a very limited conception of freedom. Countries with established churches may guarantee what they call "religious liberty," but at best it is religious toleration, and it was James Madison who said that "the right of every man is to liberty—not toleration."[4] We in the United States believe that we have the fullest religious liberty. We enjoy this religious liberty primarily because of the provision in our constitution for the separation of church and state. This means, among other things, that any threat to our separation theory is a threat to religious liberty.

We believe that religious liberty, when properly defined and understood, provides for freedom of worship, conscience, and association. This means that the individual is free to believe or not to believe, to worship or not to worship, to associate or not to associate with others of his religious persuasion. He is free to share his religious experiences, opinions, and convictions so long as he does not violate the rights of others. These basic rights of the individual belong to him within the Christian community as well as in the world. This means, among other things, that the threat to religious liberty can come from within the church and denomination as well as from a secularist world.

When religious liberty is properly interpreted, it also provides for the freedom of the Christian community to gather for purposes of evangelizing, teaching, and worship. It will have the right of propaganda not only within its own ranks but also in the world. These rights must be exercised with proper regard for the rights of others. Freedom for the Christian community also means freedom from external control due to any financial, political, or other connection with any political entity.

This means that when we talk about the secularist threat to religious liberty we should consider this liberty from the perspective of the individual Christian and also from the viewpoint of the Christian community.

SECULARISM: PAST AND PRESENT

Secularism is not exclusively a modern phenomenon. It is grounded basically in the nature of man, in his proclivity to exalt himself to the place that properly belongs to God. The contemporary expression of secularism stems, to a considerable degree, from the Renaissance, which represented, among other things, a revival of Greek learning. The humanism which was a product of the Renaissance was more or less theocentric at the beginning, but it naturally and inevitably became more and more anthropocentric. In other words, it became less Christian and more secular. This development, which some prefer to label "the Renaissance in decline," has provided the dominant tone of the contemporary world, even being predominant in some phases of theological thought.

It should be said that the Renaissance, along with the Reformation, won the independence of man from the control of the dead hand of a sterile ecclesiasticism. This freedom released tremendous creative energies in the arts, in science, in business, and even in religion. There was latent in the freedom, however, an unwholesome independence and self-assertiveness in the various areas. The arts, science, business, and other areas tended to become laws unto themselves, recognizing no external or absolute source of authority over them. Asserting their independence of the eccelesiastical authority, they tended, sooner or later, to assert their independence of God Himself. This meant that since man is by nature in rebellion against God, there was an inevitable tendency in the Renaissance toward secular self-sufficiency.

There are other contributing factors, such as the industrial revolution, to the growth and spread of secularism, but whatever its sources, we are now in a secularist age. The Dean of Harvard Divinity School, in his relatively recent Lyman Beecher Lectures, said that this secularist age "proclaims itself frankly, proudly, even a bit boisterously."[5] It is possible, of course, that its boisterousness is an evidence of its uncertainty. At least Herbert Butterfield, the famous English historian, claims that secularism is unhappy, "flitting like a lost soul in the world," and "tragically unsure of itself."[6] It may or may not be unsure of itself, but it has largely taken over our world, including our churches. It is a threat to religious liberty and many other values that we hold dear. Our world operates in most areas without paying much attention to God and religion, except in a most casual way. One writer suggests that religious faith "has been put into a pocket to which the world may revert at odd times when and if it pleases."[7] It is no longer a pervasive element in our national life, and we sometimes wonder if it is even so within our churches. As secular humanism, secularism has become a competing religion.

Samuel Miller has described our contemporary secularistic age in a most striking way. He says,

> It has more power, but scarcely more control. It has gained knowledge, but to a large degree lost wisdom. . . . It travels with speed . . . but it lacks direction and penetration. . . . It has few or no ideals and yet it is incurably optimistic. In technics it is incredibly ingenious, in politics unbelievably paranoid, and in religion hopelessly infantile.[8]

It is a world in which "nobody knows where the sun is going to rise, a world where . . . everybody is late and going nowhere in a hurry; where everybody dreads the future, has no time for the past, and wears a mask in order to see as little as possible of the present."[9]

This may be overdrawn, to a degree, as is frequently true when picturesque language is used to describe anything. Nevertheless, it portrays in general the kind of world that challenges our churches and threatens our liberties.

SECULARISM, SEPARATION, AND RELIGIOUS LIBERTY

There are some who contend that the major problem in our
country is not secularism but our theory of the separation of
church and state, particularly as that theory is interpreted by
many citizens. It is contended that secularism itself is a product of
our separation theory. Admittedly, when the separation theory is
interpreted to mean the separation of religion and the state, this
will contribute to the secularization of life. Unfortunately, some
friends as well as enemies of religious liberty have so interpreted
the separation theory. However, the separation of church and
state basically means an organizational and functional separation.
Neither is to interfere with the other in its distinctive functions or
seek to control the other.

When separation is properly understood, it is clear that it is
not responsible for secularism. After all, secularism was in existence long before our nation, with its separation theory. And it is
as prevalent, if not more so, in other nations that do not provide
for the separation of church and state.

The real threat to religious liberty does not come from separation, as some people imply, but from secularism. Micklem correctly says that it is "the loss . . . of that which counts as of
supreme value in the nature of man, his personal dignity and freedom, which is threatened by what we have called the rising tide
of secularism."[10] The fruit of a secular humanism, which theoretically exalts man apart from God, is to debase him or at best to
depersonalize him. This is seen most clearly in communism,
which, along with other secular regimes, is the fullest institutional
embodiment of secularist trends. Man in the mass may be exalted,
but man the individual has few if any rights. He is an instrument
to be used in the promotion of the Party program.

Furthermore, however loud may be the pronouncement regarding separation of church and state in a totalitarian regime, the
church's rights are definitely limited. The tendency is to use the
church as well as the individual as an instrument. The church
may be "free" as long as it does what the state wants or does not

challenge the state. Let us not conclude too quickly that we are completely free of this tendency in our own country. Politicians and political parties tend to use the church.

The threat of secularism to man and his liberty and to the church and its freedom is particularly acute when and where it has become a religion. And secularism has become a religion, at least to some degree, not only in communist and other totalitarian countries, but also in our country. If it were neutral religiously, it would not create such serious problems, but as John Bennett has suggested, our secularist religion became a problem "as it developed a pretentious ideology that offered its own answers to religious questions."[11] Bennett also states that this pretension is particularly dangerous in public schools. There is a possibility that this fourth religion—secular humanism—may enjoy rights and liberties, particularly in the schools, that are not accorded our historic faiths. This is a threat to religious liberty and to our whole way of life. Let us be careful that we do not deny the Jew, the Catholic, the Protestant the right to propagate his faith, while permitting the secular humanist the fullest of freedom.

It is possible that believers in religious freedom may be trapped by the secularists. They may join the latter in carrying the separation theory further than our founding fathers intended. While we properly may not defend certain formal and official expressions of religion in public life, we should defend to the last the right of a Christian to be a Christian wherever he is: in the classroom, in the legislative hall, in his office or place of business, anywhere. This means, among other things, that while we may not be disturbed about the elimination of compulsory Bible reading and formal prayers in the classroom, we should at the same time be deeply concerned that more Christian men and women, with a sense of divine purpose, will dedicate themselves to public school teaching. And when they get into the classroom, we should hope and pray that they will be wholesomely and positively Christian. The same could be said for men and women in business, in politics, and in every other area of life.

Democracy defends the right of the citizen to seek to influence society in harmony with his ideas of the good life. He has the right wherever he is to pass on the Christian perspective. Let us not let the secularists rob us of this basic right. Certainly the Christian should always have a proper regard for the rights and privileges of others.

THE CHURCH, THE WORLD, AND RELIGIOUS LIBERTY

A more insidious and hence more dangerous threat to religious liberty comes from secularism within our churches. It is Davies who says that "church members are only a degree less secularized . . . than the public that is completely divorced from the Church."[12] What Davies says concerning church members could also be said regarding the church as such. It is little less secularized than the culture surrounding it. Many of our churches identify themselves with and have become defenders of the culture. While we decry *establishment*, such as is found in European countries, we have tended to slip into what Franklin Littell calls "social establishment."

The secularization of the church expresses itself in various and even contradictory ways. The church uses, to a distressing degree, secular methods to attain worldly success. The greatness of a local church is frequently measured by the number of its members, the improvement of its physical facilities, and the size of its budget. One result of this kind of emphasis is that there are evidently many unredeemed people in our churches, with the rest of us considerably less mature than we should be. In turn, the unredeemed and the immature are a constant threat to religious liberty in the world and in the church. There can be no assurance of the preservation of religious liberty in our nation apart from churches composed of redeemed, spiritually maturing men and women who will defend the right and accept the responsibility of religious liberty.

Let us repeat—the thing that has created the real problem in our churches has been their secularization, their desire for success from the secular perspective. The latter is one reason why so many insist that everything must run smoothly. It is expected in many churches, particularly the larger, "more successful ones," that every recommendation from the pastor, deacons, or any committee will be accepted without any questions. There is little liberty to differ, at least publicly. Religious liberty is largely lost within the house of her "friends." How can we expect to preserve it in the nation and the world if we do not preserve it within the company of the redeemed?

Miller, speaking from the perspective of the minister, suggests that he "finds himself in a nasty jam," and incidentally a jam that some ministers seem thoroughly to enjoy. He suggests that unless the minister

> plays the game, promotes success, snags new members, . . . keeps the program humping, . . . opens up new resources . . . , oils the works with suavity and poise, plays the impresario with all the organizations, increases the congregation and ups the budget—then by every rule of thumb in current use his name is mud, not only as far as the local church is concerned, but as well with the bureaucracy that controls the next step up the ladder on the basis of the record.[13]

Paradoxically, while the church tends to measure its success in secular terms, it also tends to withdraw from the world. For example, being a Christian is frequently considered to be what one does within the walls of a church building on Sunday. One wonders sometimes if our church buildings have been primarily a blessing or a curse. They represent at times, as Kierkegaard says, "an artistic remoteness from reality."[14] At least, to use an expression of David Jenkins, our churches should not "make totalitarian claims for the service of the sanctuary." They should seek to ensure "that the Church maintains her vital rhythm of gathering and scattering, of withdrawal and engagement."[15] The same author also suggests that the church is an army on the march, with its ordinary members as the front-line troops engaged with the world. The Christian minister's task is to help them to be fit for battle.

Some churches with fine church buildings have attempted to domesticate God. They tend to be self-centered and in love with themselves. Their members are frequently pharisaical in their attitudes toward those outside the Christian fellowship—the very ones who need most the message that the church has to deliver. While it is true that Christ died for the church, it is also true that God so loved the world that He gave His only begotten Son. Our God is not exclusively the God of the church; He is also creatively active in the world. If we limit our Christian witness to the church building, we shall contribute to the further seculariation of our world and hence to the threat of our religious liberty. What is needed desperately in our world is a church composed of dynamically redeemed individuals who will recognize that the church is wherever they are on Monday through Saturday, as well as on Sunday.

It has been implied previously that the secular credo of success not only plagues the local church but also the church in general, or the denomination. Many denominational leaders tend not only to measure the success of the local church and pastor in secular terms; they also tend to do the same thing for themselves, the denomination, and its program. One indication of this was the craze a few years ago for studies of denominational programs by efficiency experts. These studies doubtlessly did some good, but they were another evidence of the impact of the secular on our work. Still another evidence is the salary scale of some of our agencies with the salary differentials determined largely on a secular basis.

Still another evidence of the influence of the secular is the fact that many denominational leaders believe that something is drastically wrong if evangelistic results, gifts to financial programs, and other materially measurable results do not consistently increase. They fail to see that a slowdown or a decrease may be due to the fact that secular methods have been used largely to achieve secular results. Such methods tend sooner or later to exhaust themselves. Our churches and denominations need to reevaluate every aspect of the program and restudy methods. We may discover that we will need to place more emphasis on the quality of work rather than on the quantity of results. We may also discover that we cannot have the quantity indefinitely unless we improve the quality.

The desire for secular success by denominational leaders poses a threat to religious liberty from a different perspective. A great denomination, measured by the standards of the world, cannot be built without unity. Unfortunately, unity is frequently equated with uniformity. Hence, many times there is not the freedom there should be for pastors, laymen, or even churches to disagree with denominational programs or leadership. This posits a real threat not only to religious liberty but also to the vitality of the Christian movement.

In addition, there is the threat that stems from the fact that many leaders tend to judge the success of the denomination by the number and size of the institutions or agencies owned and operated by it. Many of those agencies and institutions, in turn, are trying to be as big as possible. The denominational conventions or conferences are unable to support them adequately. What will be done: will some institutions be consolidated or liquidated? The answer in most cases is "no"—nothing will be done, although in some cases something should be done. Actually, most church and denominational bodies are constantly increasing the number and size of their institutions.

The pressure must be terrific on the administrative heads of many of those institutions or agencies. They cannot get enough funds from the denomination. If they increase their charges too much, tuition or otherwise, they may price themselves out of business, or at least be unable to reach and minister to the people who need them most. One temptation, under such conditions, is to turn to good old generous Uncle Sam for a gift or at least a loan. This means a weakening of the wall of separation and hence constitutes a threat to religious liberty: the liberty of the institution, the denomination, the church, and the individual.

The temptation for institutional administrators is increased at times by the attitude of some denominational leaders. The desire of the latter for secular success tends to dull their sensitivity to the danger of governmental aid of any kind.

CONCLUSION: THE WAY AHEAD

What can we do to guard against the secularist threat to religious liberty in our nation, our world, and our churches?

What can the denomination and denominational leaders do to protect religious liberty?

1. Our leaders should seek to provide a broad base for religious liberty within the life, work, and program of the churches and the denomination, protecting the right to participate in the democratic processes within the churches and the denomination.

2. The denomination, and that includes all of us, should be satisfied to have only the institutions we can adequately support without adversely affecting our mission outreach at home and around the world. This may mean fewer and smaller institutions, but let us hope that every institution we support will be thoroughly Christian, freed from the insidious enslavement to secularistic hopes, goals, and methods.

3. Our leaders should rethink and encourage our people to rethink our programs and methods throughout the entire church. We may find that under the pressure of our secularist culture we have been moving in unwise and ultimately self-defeating ways.

What can the churches do?

1. They can seek to maintain or recapture a regenerated church membership, exercising more care in admitting members, being more concerned for their maturity, and reactivating in some form proper church discipline.

2. The churches should protect and defend the right of the prophet in the pulpit or the pew.

3. The church should truly be the church of God, recognizing Christ alone as its head. It "is not *of* the world," although it "is in the world" and "for the world."[16]

4. The church should know that spiritual separation from the world, coupled with active participation in the life of the world, will create tension not only between the church and the secular world but also within the very soul of the church itself.

5. The church needs to practice what it preaches, particularly its message of self-denial and cross-bearing. It is in the world to minister, not to be ministered to. A secularist world would like for it to be a private affair, a religious club, removed from public life. This it cannot be and still be the church of God doing the work of God in His world.

What can we personally do about the secularist threat to religious liberty?

1. We need to think through as clearly as possible our own position regarding the separation of church and state and religious liberty in the church and the world.

2. We should examine our own values and perspectives to see how much we have been influenced by secularist concepts and ideals.

3. We should remember that ours is not a Christian nation. It, and our world in general, is influenced much more by secular humanism than by vital Christianity.

4. Regardless of how much we find wrong in our churches and in our particular denomination, we should remain unquestionably loyal. William Stringfellow tells about a Frenchman who said that the dilemma Christians faced in France was that the church had become "so debilitated and apostate that a Christian" could "hardly bear to remain in a church, and yet . . . no Christian" could leave the church "lest he fail to confess his own part of the responsibility for the very conditions" which provoked his protest.[17] We cannot escape involvement in and responsibility for the shortcomings and sins of our churches. If they have become secularized, it is because we and others like us are secular in our thinking and perspective.

5. Let each one of us be sure that he gives the same freedom or liberty to others that he desires for himself.

Chapter 15

REFLECTIONS REGARDING DEMOCRACY

Have you ever seen a large religious convention in action? Did the discussion at the convention reveal the strength, the weakness, or both the strength and weakness of democracy? When is a meeting in a church, an association, or a convention a "good church meeting"? Is it necessarily a good meeting when there is not a dissenting voice or vote? Or, is it more likely to be a "good church meeting" when differing viewpoints are freely expressed and following adequate discussion a decision is made by a majority vote? How is the contemporary theological discussion or controversy related to our democratic way of life? Is there a possibility that a church's or a denomination's democracy may be endangered by an effort to preserve its orthodoxy? These questions have been asked without any intention of answering them.

Even though the concern of this discussion is primarily democracy in the church, the insights of secular historians, philosophers, and political scientists will be utilized. This will be done for two main reasons: (1) Comparatively little has been written on democracy in the church in contrast to an abundance of material on political democracy. (2) Many of the principles and problems of democracy in the state are strikingly similar to the principles and problems of democracy in the church. This means that much of what the scholars say regarding political democracy is just as applicable to religious democracy.

It possibly should be suggested at this point that there is a very real sense in which our churches are not democracies but Christocracies. Christ is the head of the church. His will is to be done by the church. His voice is authoritative for and in the church. But how and through whom does Christ reveal His will to the church? Rightly or wrongly, wisely or unwisely, the democratic faith is that the Holy Spirit reveals the way and will of Christ for the church to the entire membership rather than to any individual (pastor or anyone else) or small group within the church family, such as the deacons or a committee. This kind of faith is closely related to and is derived from certain fundamental principles or basic concepts of democracy.

BASIC CONCEPTS

Some of these concepts that are usually considered primarily political are just as applicable to the church as to the state. For example, Lincoln's succinct statement, which is really a definition of democracy, has considerable relevance for our churches. He described our government as "a government of the people, by the people, and for the people." Ralph Barton Perry somewhat similarly says that American democracy "is a union of two independent theories: a theory as to the value or good for the sake of which the state exists, and a theory as to the seat of the control which the state exercises."[1] The same author also makes a distinction between what he terms "social democracy" and "political democracy." The former answers the question about the purpose of government—it is the "for" the people; the latter answers the question about the form of government that will best achieve that purpose—it is the "of" and "by" the people.

There are some insights in the preceding paragraph that will help us to understand the operation and some of the problems of democracy in our churches as well as in the state. For example, institutions and agencies, including both the church and state, exist "for the people." There is a strong conviction in our democratic dream concerning the worth and dignity of the individual person. This means from the perspective of our churches that he is to be kept central in everything we do. Programs and organizations are never to be ends in themselves but always means or methods to serve the people. A deep conviction and a consistent practice at this point would go a long way toward solving some of our most difficult problems.

The people to whom the church ministers are both equal and unequal. There is a sense in which all men are created equal, but also a sense in which they are unequal. They are unequal in ability, in maturity, in influence, and in power, but they are equal in all that makes them distinctly men. They are equally citizens of the state or members of the church. They have certain inalienable rights. For example, within the church fellowship each member has an equal right to express his opinion and to cast his vote in determining the policies of the church.

Another important concept is that in a democracy decisions are made by the people. Not only is authority in a democracy derived from, or is "of the people"; it is also exercised "by the people." Thomas Jefferson never tired of saying, "The mass of the people is the safest depository of their own rights." He also said, "No government can continue good but under the control of the people."[2] Since unanimity is frequently lacking, the majority in a democracy has the right to make decisions for the entire group. Rule by a majority is safe only if majority decisions are based on reason and good will and are motivated by a desire to serve all the people. This is just as true in the church as it is in the state. When majority rule "is combined with an agreement to differ and with the principle of compromise," democracy will be saved from the tyranny of the majority.[3]

In other words, democracy is government by discussion. In the process each individual must be free to state and defend his opinion. Decisions are "by persuasion and arbitration,"[4] and are never "regarded as irrevocable."[5] The last idea is particularly important in the church. The majority may be wrong. Majority decision should not be equated with the will of God, nor even the voice of all the people with the voice of God. This means that decision-making in a church should be a continuous process. There should be an element of tentativeness about most decisions. There will be a constant interplay of differing viewpoints. The rights of the minority must be protected—not only the right to be heard but also the right to seek through persuasion to become the majority. In other words, a healthy democracy in a church, as in the state, combines majority rule with the protection of minority rights. This majority rule must be an "expression of reasoned judgment" rather than "an expression of will,"[6] or the result of the press of numbers, or prestige. If it is the latter, it will be majority dictatorship and democracy will be destroyed. The rights of the minority will not and cannot be properly protected unless there is freedom of speech, press, and assembly. These are just as essential for democracy in the church as in the state.

Another basic concept of democracy is that leadership arises from the people and is selected and elected by the people. Democracy in church or state, but particularly in the former, is threatened when those in places of leadership have sought those places rather than having been sought for them.

It is also true that the leader in a democracy is to speak "for the people," which does not necessarily mean that he will always say what the people want him to say. Rather, he is to speak on behalf of, or in the best interest of, the people. He is to consider the welfare of all the people and not any one segment or group. He is to recognize that his responsibility reaches beyond his immediate constituency, whether that is a political district or a church. First consideration must be given to the people as a whole, and from the Christian perspective it must be for the cause of Christ. His primary responsibility, whether he serves in state or church, is to God. The latter will make the leader more concerned about the welfare of the people. He will tend to become a political or religious statesman rather than a mere politician. If he is the latter, he can rather easily become a demagogue, and there are religious as well as political demagogues. The Christian statesman or prophet hears the voice of God above the voice of the people. He speaks the word of God to the people, but that word is always spoken for the good of the people.

Another characteristic of democracy is that it is an open rather than a closed society. The people have an opportunity to know about failures as well as successes. The difference between an open and a closed society has been demonstrated quite clearly in recent years in the contrast between the way the space and missile program has been handled in the United States and in the Soviet Union. The fact that a democracy is an open society has considerable significance for churches, denominations, and their agencies and institutions. If we are to preserve our democracy, decisions must be made openly and reports concerning the status of the work must be readily available. This applies to every aspect of the work, including the items in the budget for a local church, an association, a convention, or its agencies. Insofar as salaries and other items are covered up the church or agency is operating as a closed rather than an open society. Some of the unrest in churches and denominations stems from a conviction that this is being done in some areas and to some degree.

Before we discuss in a more specific way some additional problems of democracy, let us in outline form suggest some personal qualities that are essential for the effective operation of a democracy. These qualities are needed by the people in general and by their leaders. Among the more important of these are: (1) A relatively high level of intelligence in general and of political intelligence in particular. From the church's perspective "political intelligence" includes a knowledge of distinctive beliefs and an acquaintance with the way churches and denominations are supposed to operate. (2) The capacity to distinguish between the important and the unimportant, the essential and the nonessential, with a willingness to compromise on non-essentials and through discussion and persuasion to seek a workable agreement on essentials. (3) A spirit of goodwill and of basic honesty, joined with a magnanimous spirit which gives one the ability to see the other person's viewpoint and to accept defeat graciously. (4) A devotion to the common good. (5) A spirit of tolerance coupled with a high degree of self-discipline. (6) The ability to disagree agreeably, combined with a basic respect for those with whom one differs. This means that there will be relatively little name calling or the use of labels, which is usually an evidence of one's inability to answer his opponent. The need for these and additional qualities is quite evident in the present period of self-examination and soul-searching by churches and denominations. Insofar as they are lacking, our democracy, from the Christian perspective, is threatened.

CONTINUING PROBLEMS

Let us now shift our attention to a more specific consideration of some of the major problems of democracy. In doing so, we shall consider the following questions relative to the basic concepts discussed previously: (1) Are we in danger in church and state of drifting away from or losing our faith in the fundamental principles that are essential to the democratic way of life? (2) Are these basic concepts valid and hence is democracy founded on a realistic or an unrealistic faith? For example, is the democratic faith in the basic goodness of man and in his capacity to govern himself fact or fiction? Possibly most of us would agree with Hallowell that democracy's faith in man as a rational, moral, and spiritual creature "is as much aspiration as it is fact."[7] Rather typically, Reinhold Niebuhr suggests that "the excessively optimistic estimate of human nature and of human history with which the democratic credo has been historically associated is a source of peril to democratic society."[8]

It is doubtful if there is a sound basis for political democracy where there is lacking a vital Christian movement. This is one reason why many so-called political democracies have failed.

Where the people are lacking in intelligence and in an unselfish devotion to the common good, democracy slips very easily into anarchy, and anarchy in turn is fallow ground for the rise of a dictatorship.

While the danger of anarchy is not as evident in the church as in the state, it is present to some degree. At least democracy in the church is endangered by unregenerate and spiritually immature church members. If we are concerned with the preservation of democracy in our churches, we should be careful about the admission of members into the churches, and we should be vitally concerned about their growth and maturity once they become members. The threat from immaturity comes from leadership as well as from the rank and file of the people. Few things threaten democracy more in the church or in a denomination than for the leadership to be in the hands of selfish, grasping individuals who are dominated by a will for power. There should be no place in our life, in the churches, or in the denominations, for a dictator. There is a fine line of distinction, but a very important one, between positive leadership and dictatorship.

When the people are immature and poorly prepared for self-government, and at the same time there are among them some who are grasping for leadership, the democratic process itself may be used to destroy democracy. In other words, through a majority vote the people may approve a government or a plan that will deprive them of the privilege of governing themselves. This has been done in the political area in the past; it will doubtless be done in the future. Those who rise to leadership in such a situation appeal primarily to the prejudices of the people rather than to their intelligence. While this is more of a problem in political than in religious circles, it may be more prevalent in the latter than many of us realize. At least to the degree that the people in our churches are unredeemed and immature, they can be swayed by an appeal to prejudice rather than by an appeal to think and do right. There are at least a few so-called leaders who do not hesitate to make that appeal. This helps to explain the fact that sometimes the popularly elected leaders of churches and particularly of denominations are not the best qualified men and women. It should be stated parenthetically that one reason for this is the fact that many of our best qualified men, to use their own words, will not get mixed up in denominational politics.

Closely akin to, and as implied, one reason for the preceding problem is the failure of many of our people to accept the responsibilities that democracy entails. Just as one of the chief threats to political democracy is the poor citizenship of good people, so one of the chief problems of religious democracy is the poor churchmanship of so many good Christian people. And incidentally, if democracy is lost in the denomination it will be because it is first lost in the local churches. There are entirely too many church members who rather than think through a church problem prefer to leave the decision to the pastor or a committee. This attitude may become so prevalent that it will be difficult for anyone to speak regarding any recommendation brought to the church. If he does, he will be considered queer or an obstructionist.

The problems so far discussed are more or less inherent in the democratic process. There are, on the other hand, some problems that have arisen in our churches and denominations largely because of contemporary developments and trends. One such development is the bigness of so many of our churches and denominations—their agencies and institutions. The bigger and the more complex the operation, the more difficult it is to use established democratic processes. For example, the old town meeting was the purest expression of democracy in political life.

The tendency in the large church is for decisions to be made by the pastor, the church staff, or/and a few "top-level leaders" and then handed down to the remainder of the congregation. This tendency is more prevalent in the denomination where the development of a bureaucracy of some proportion seems more or less inevitable. Many of the bureaucrats may be our good friends, but bureaucracy in church or state is a threat to democracy.

One thing that has been a contributing factor to dictatorship or bureaucratic control in churches and denominations has been our emphasis on success. And success has been measured almost exclusively in worldly material terms. If democratic processes are inefficient or slow, the tendency has been to abandon them. This emphasis on success affects not only the church and the denomination but also the leadership of both. For example, a pastor or a minister of education is under pressure to show measurable results. He may reason that he knows better than the people what is required to grow a church, which in most cases will be correct. Since this is true, why should he not make the necessary decisions? One thing that he may forget is that when he bypasses the people he may "grow a church," but he will not develop its members into morally and spiritually mature individuals.

There are many other unfortunate aspects of this credo of success, of which only one will be mentioned here. Some pastors have a strong desire to gain the recognition and approval of denominational leaders. They know that these leaders may determine, to a considerable degree, their places of service in the future. And after all, they would like to have some place of leadership in the denomination. Some of them seem at times to be willing to sell their integrity if not their souls for a mess of denominational pottage. This was evidently true of a young minister who said, "I want to get ahead in the denomination. Anything my denomination and its leaders say is all right with me." If this attitude becomes common among our pastors it will undermine the very foundations of democracy. The prophetic spirit may be like a thorn in the flesh to the leadership of a democracy, but it is very necessary to its health and vitality.

What will democracy do, to use an Arnold Toynbee expression, with its creative minority? Ortega y Gassett possibly goes too far when he says that in the United States "to be different is to be indecent,"[9] but there is some pressure toward the leveling of people in a religious as well as in a political democracy.

There seems to be an almost innate tendency in a democracy to neutralize outstanding ability. After all, creative ability is a disturbing factor in society because it usually challenges the old ways. In any society, religious or political, where the powers that be have set themselves to maintain the status quo, the creative individual frequently will be considered a traitor or a heretic. A healthy democracy, however, is never static, never a defender as such of the status quo. It must be a dynamic movement, adjustable to new insights and new problems, although admittedly it is slow to change.

There is still another problem that we must consider. It is of such significance that this entire chapter could have been devoted to it. It is a problem that is inherent in democracy in both church and state. It is the proper uniting and balancing of freedom and responsibility. Hallowell makes a distinction between two competing conceptions of freedom: (1) freedom to do what one wants to do, and (2) what he terms freedom to serve God and one's fellowman. The first "regards power as an end in itself; the other as a means to promote justice and the common good."[10]

The first is freedom without responsibility, the second is freedom coupled with responsibility. Carl Becker says that these two —freedom and responsibility—cannot be discussed or dealt with to any good purpose separately. He further says, "Freedom unrestrained by responsibility becomes mere license, responsibility unchecked by freedom becomes mere arbitrary power. The question, then, is not whether freedom and responsibility shall be united, but how they can be united and reconciled to the best advantage."[11]

It does not take a seer to see the application of the preceding to some of the developments and trends in our churches and denominations. We believe, for example, that the pastor should be free to deliver God's message to the people, but we also believe that he should have a deep sense of responsibility to God and to the people. He should be sure that it is God's message that he delivers, but he should also be sure that it is delivered in the spirit of understanding and love. In turn, the church has both some rights or freedoms and responsibilities. In other words, there are freedoms or rights and responsibilities on both sides of this relationship.

The same thing is true when the perspective is broadened to the denomination. The denominational worker or leader in the classroom or anywhere else should be free, but united with the freedom should be a deep sense of personal responsibility. Without this sense of responsibility his freedom will tend to deteriorate into license. There should be a supreme sense of responsibility to God and to the truth, but there should also be a genuine sense of responsibility to the denomination and to those one serves. This means, among other things, that the teacher or leader, as is true of the pastor, should recognize the importance of the way he says a thing as well as what he says. As one who is supposed to be more mature, he should seek to speak in such a way as to stabilize and strengthen the faith of the less mature rather than to weaken or to destroy that faith. He has a responsibility to share his deeper insights into the truth with them, but he should do this in such a way and in such a spirit as to enable them to incorporate these insights into a richer, a more mature, and a more meaningful faith.

Let us repeat that rights and responsibilities are a two-way street. Agencies and institutions have some rights as well as those who serve in and through them. However, those agencies and institutions along with their boards and administrative staffs also should have a proper sense of their responsibility to those employed by them and to the denomination.

One of the very real problems for Baptists in this whole area is that they do not have any clear-cut authority that can determine the limits of freedom. What are the things one must believe to be a Baptist? Where can he find the "orthodox line"? After all, how much room is there within our ranks for differing opinions? May we get so narrow in our orthodoxy that we undermine our belief in the competency of the individual person?

Is it not possible that freedom to differ has been one secret to the vitality of the Baptist movement? Should there not be freedom within our denomination to discuss objectively and dispassionately various issues and problems that disturb us? Do we not have enough faith in our people and in truth to believe that truth will ultimately triumph among us? Can we not be mature enough to concentrate on the issues and quit name-calling?

On the other hand, what about those who seek greater freedom? Are they using wisely and constructively the freedom they have? Why do they want more freedom? Do they have the right to expect additional freedom if they are not unquestionably loyal to the denomination and thoroughly committed to its welfare?

Just as this chapter was opened with a series of questions that were not answered, so it is closed with the preceding unanswered questions. You, I, and others must answer these and many related questions. The answers will determine, to a considerable degree, the future of our churches, of our denominations, and of democracy within our churches and denominations.

Chapter 16

THIS REVOLUTIONARY WORLD

"The succession of crises has become constant and perpetual," so much so that "men live in a continuous state of emergency that they are coming to accept as normal."[1] This "continuous state of emergency" is particularly prevalent in Asia, Africa, and Latin America. The president of Chile recently said, "Our first duty is with a world emerging in history in search of a path and expression."[2]

It is this emerging world, a world in search of a path or direction and still seeking ways to express itself, that challenges missionaries and all of us who are concerned about world missions. Missionaries go to their fields with the same Christ in their hearts and the same basic message on their lips as their predecessors, but they go to a drastically different world. This changing revolutionary world may demand new strategies and different methods to achieve the same ends.

The purpose of this chapter is to describe the rapid social, economic, and political changes, particularly during the last decade, that have a direct bearing upon the status of Christianity in the world and the possibility of carrying on a foreign mission enterprise. It is my feeling that a restudy and reevaluation of the missionary enterprise is demanded by current conditions.

NATURE OF THE REVOLUTION

It does not take a prophet to know that ours is a revolutionary world. Many students of world affairs consider the present revolution the most serious the world has known since the days of the Renaissance and Reformation. It reaches into every area of the world.

One cannot understand the contemporary revolutionary world unless he understands something of the nature of cultures and civilizations. They are built or unified around a central core of values. When that central core is disturbed, a crisis is created. This crisis is accompanied by chaos and confusion, which will continue until the center is reintegrated or a new center is formed. The period between the disturbance of the center of the culture or civilization and when it is reintegrated, or a new center is created, can properly be called a revolution. The revolution may be violent or nonviolent.

The unifying center of a culture or civilization can be disturbed and fail to be an effectively integrating center because of competition from without or decay from within. The latter is the usual process in a stronger or a more advanced civilization.

One way to describe, in broad outline, what has happened in our world is to point out that the more highly industrialized nations of the West have gone around the world in search of raw materials and markets for their manufactured products. As their representatives have gone, more or less inevitably some of the ideas and ideals or central concepts of Western civilization have gone along. In other words, as Western nations have exported their goods and techniques, they have inescapably exported some of their values.

The crises or revolutions in Asia, Africa, Latin America, and elsewhere cannot be understood apart from their contact with the nations of the North Atlantic community or what has been termed "Western civilization." The integrating centers of these cultures have been disturbed, if not destroyed, by their contact with and competition from the basic values of Western civilization. Crises have been created for them which will persist until their existing unifying centers are either revived and reintegrated, or until they appropriate enough of the values of Western civilization to have a new integrating center.

At the very time when Western civilization has exported its basic concepts to other parts of the world, it finds itself in a major crisis period. This crisis in the West stems primarily from the inner decay of its integrating center. This could be expressed in a number of ways, but possibly as accurate and pointed as any would be to say that Western civilization, to a distressing degree, has lost its faith. This loss of faith could be spelled out in different ways, but most meaningful from our perspective here is the fact that the West has lost its enthusiasm, if not its faith, in its way of life.

What John Macmurray said concerning Great Britain could be said regarding many of the peoples of other Western nations. He said he did not know anything that the British were enthusiastic about any more. Emile Caillett has a chapter entitled "The Lost Radiance" in one of his books. The chapter refers to Western civilization, which has lost its radiance. Trueblood speaks of ours as a "cut-flower civilization." A cut-flower has been separated from the source of its strength and vitality—it soon withers and dies.

This suggests that the contemporary revolution, which is basically spiritual—a crisis regarding central integrating values—is also worldwide in its scope. Everywhere the Christian missionary goes, he will face a localized crisis or revolution, which cannot be understood apart from its relation to the broader world revolution. In other words, there are *revolutions* and yet *a revolution*. It is the latter that gives some degree of meaning and unity to the more or less isolated revolutions. To use an expression of Tillich, which represents a somewhat different perspective, there is "a single revolutionary vortex."[3] The revolutions in various parts of the world are expressions of or, from Tillich's perspective, are drawn into the world revolution.

CONTRIBUTORS TO THE REVOLUTION

There are a number of factors that have contributed in different ways and to varying degrees to the contemporary world revolution. This section will be restricted to a relatively brief statement concerning a few of these factors.

Science has contributed in many ways to the revolutionary nature of our world. Halle, in the article previously cited, suggests that the power of mankind, including the power to destroy, has gone up steadily until in our time the curve that describes the increase has suddenly approximated the vertical. From nothing but his own muscular power, man has moved through the domestication of animals, the perfection of water mills and windmills, the discovery of steam power, to the release of the practically infinite power hitherto locked up in the atom.

Possibly more directly related to the world revolution is the accelerated pace of improvements in transportation, which is another contribution of science to the contemporary world revolution. These improvements have tended to make any major problem anywhere in the world a problem for the whole world— a global problem. The curve representing progress in this area seems to be approaching the vertical. We are now in the jet age. An experimental plane for commercial use has already been tested that exceeded 2,000 miles per hour at an altitude of 70,000 feet. It has been suggested that we can cross the Atlantic in two hours in the near future. And there are the fantastic days ahead of manned space vehicles and even the possibility of interplanetary travel.

Most significant in many ways for those of us who are involved in and concerned about our world mission enterprise is the rapid change in means of communication. Without outlining the progress step by step, just think of the radio and television, both of which have first been made available in the lifetime of many of us. The satellite age came with Telstar I and "The Early Bird," the first commercial satellite. The latter remains stationary 22,300 miles above the equator of the earth. Actually, in order to remain stationary in relation to the earth, it has to move at the rate of 7,000 miles per hour. "The Early Bird," sometimes called "Comsat" (Commercial Satellite), will carry at one time as many as 240 telephone conversations. It can also be used for two-way television. It makes it possible for everyone to keep an eye on everything.

Halle concludes that "with the upswing in curves approaching the vertical, we find ourselves rushed along at a headlong pace that confronts us with a challenge unlike any we have faced before."[4] Our churches dare not continue to *do business as usual* or they will be left beside the road. The same is true of missionary work around the world. When everything else is accelerating, we must accelerate what we are doing if we are to speak to the needs of a revolutionary world. We need to utilize more effectively than we have the improved means of transportation and communication in the spread of the Gospel. At the same time, we should guard against the possibility that these improved means will cause us to live more removed and isolated from the masses, resulting in an impersonal approach.

The acceleration of man's power to destroy should provide an unusual sense of urgency for our missionary task at home and around the world. Science and our industrial "know-how" have, as Toynbee suggests, "expanded all human operations, including genocide, to a world-wide scale." There are now available fifty to one hundred megaton bombs, one of which could destroy millions of people. Toynbee correctly says that "the slaughterhouse is global, and it is now all set for instant use." He further says that "a bomb with an atomic warhead could be delivered from any point on or above the earth's surface, or in adjoining outer space, to any other point on the earth's surface." He does suggest, however, that a potential global slaughterhouse can be transformed into a global home. Mankind can choose "between committing mass suicide and learning to live together as a single family."[5] There does not seem to be much hope for men to live as one family, except as they are brought into the family of God.

The restless movement of the masses is another major contributor to the contemporary world revolution. The pressure created by the so-called population explosion is a factor in their restlessness. There were only about 133,000,000 people in the world two thousand years ago—in the days of Jesus, and only 728,-000,000 as recently as two hundred and ten years ago. In contrast, there were 2,700,000,000 in 1960, and it is estimated that there will be 6,267,000,000 by the year 2000. There are areas of the world where this sharp increase in population creates some very serious problems for the masses of the people.

It has been said that the world owes its "onward impulses to men ill at ease." The masses of the world are ill at ease. They have been "caught up in the winds of change." They are discovering for the first time that their miseries are remediable. They are tired of promises. They want action, and they want it now. Their demand for social justice will not and cannot be denied. This movement of the masses represents what Toynbee calls the "world-revolution of the peasantry," which he considers "the most glorious revolution that there has been in the World's history so far."[6]

Frank Laubach, who doubtlessly knows the masses better than any other American, says that "they were in despair, but now they are making up their minds that they will come up—or blow up the world. They are desperate, grim, irresistible."[7] What does Laubach mean when he says the upward movement of the masses is irresistible? He evidently means that they can be guided but they cannot be stopped. Toynbee makes a similar statement concerning the world revolution in general. His statement is: "Revolution is a meddlesome horse. One must either ride it or else be trampled to death by it."[8]

What is it that the restless masses want? There seems to be at least four things: bread, or more of the good things of life; freedom; respect; and a sense of purpose. The masses may be largely unconscious of the last of these wants, but every person, created in the image of God, cannot measure up to his potential unless he has a cause or a purpose for which he is willing to die. This is written into his nature by his Creator.

The first three of the preceding wants—bread, freedom, and respect—could be summed up in the one word "justice." The masses have been conscious for some time of some of the injustices against them. In times past they rather fatalistically accepted their status. Revolution has come in our day because the masses now believe they can do something about those injustices. In seeking to correct the injustices against them, they frequently tend to turn to any man or movement that promises to give them what they want.

It is tremendously important for the missionary, and for all of us, to maintain a good rapport with the restless masses. They represent in a very real sense the wave of the future. If our Christian forces are to have an effective voice in shaping that future, they must maintain an effective witness to the masses. This is as true in the United States as it is on foreign mission fields.

The missionary frequently has the difficult task of distinguishing between the legitimate wants and needs of the restless masses and some of the methods they may use in attempting to attain their goals. Because of his desire for peace and for law and order, the missionary, if he is not careful, will find himself supporting traditional regimes that are set against the masses and their legitimate demands. He may not have the answer for the problems of the underprivileged masses, but he can at least be sympathetic with them and recognize that many of their grievances are just.

The United States, in a unique way, is a contributing factor to the contemporary world revolution. Toynbee traces the present revolution back to our American revolution. He has a chapter entitled "The Shot Heard Round the World." He claims that the shot fired at Concord is now circling the globe for the third time. He suggests, however, that the United States has reversed her role in the world. She has become affluent and has largely deserted her own revolution. It goes on without her. Her affluence has estranged her from her own ideals, and "is pushing her into becoming the policeman standing guard over vested interests."⁹ The preceding may not be a completely accurate picture, but there is enough truth in it to make us uncomfortable.

The missionary should recognize that he goes from an affluent society. This can be a considerable handicap to him in reaching the masses where he serves. The extent of the handicap will be largely determined by his personal attitude toward material things. The missionary may discover that his homeland may be a handicap to him in other ways, such as its too frequent tendency to be paternalistic toward other peoples and to identify Christianity and "the American way of life."

We should all join former President Kennedy in saying, "Let us once again awaken our American Revolution until it guides the struggles of people everywhere."

CONTEMPORARY MOVEMENTS AND THE REVOLUTION

Contemporary movements in theology, such as neo-orthodoxy, and in philosophy, such as existentialism, as well as major movements in the economic and political areas are more or less closely related to the world revolution. They are factors, at least to a limited degree, in the revolution, but primarily they are evidences or expressions of the revolution. Their popularity or growth is due to the fact that they speak to and are relevant for a world in revolution. We shall limit this portion of our study to nationalism and communism, both of which present a real challenge to the missionary movement.

As suggested earlier, one of the desires of the restless masses is freedom, freedom for the individual and for the group. This desire for freedom explains the virtual collapse of colonialism. Great Britain is a striking example. Fifteen years ago she ruled 460,000,000 people in Asia and Africa. This has decreased to 60,000,000, with the number declining constantly.

Subject peoples are no longer willing to be ruled by others.

This movement which started in the Orient in a big way a few years ago has in more recent years been running its course in Africa. About twenty-five years ago there were only two independent African countries, and as late as 1957 there were only seven. Today there are at least thirty-five. Fifteen new African nations were admitted to the United Nations in one year. Some of these may be quite small in territory, population, and economic resources, but at least they, with other noncommitted nations, provide a rather effective balance of power in the United Nations.

It is natural, if not inevitable, that the newly independent nations in Asia and Africa would be strongly nationalistic. There are also strong nationalistic movements in Latin America. One writer has said that "the most important single phenomenon in Latin America today is the rapid growth of nationalism." He also says that "the tempo of advance is quickening."[10] One reason for nationalism in Latin America is the desire of those countries to be independent of the United States. The former president of Brazil, Juscelino Kubitschek, is quoted as saying, "We want to be on the side of the West, but we do not want to be its proletariat."[11] The present nationalism in Latin America and elsewhere is popular nationalism rather than aristocratic nationalism. As such, it ties in with the march of the masses and is both an expression of and a factor in world revolution.

Because of the strength of the nationalistic feeling in many areas of the world, the missionary tends to be identified more than formerly with the nation from which he goes. He is a citizen of the United States; he is a foreigner. This explains the tendency in some places to classify the missionary movement as a foreign invasion.

One of the most perplexing and complex problems faced by the missionary on many fields is the growing self-assertedness of the national leadership in the churches. One hesitates to use a comparison, but the missionaries in some countries face a problem comparable to the one faced by the parents of teenage youngsters. When and how can they wisely shift control from themselves to the growing number of mature national leaders? It will help if they recognize that ultimately missionaries, in the main, will work under national leadership. Their work will largely be to supplement and strengthen the work of the nationals. This process has already progressed to a considerable degree in some areas. Problems arise, however, when nationals under the impact of extreme nationalism push too vigorously and prematurely for complete control of the work.

Communism, another major contemporary movement, has sought to infiltrate and utilize for its own ends nationalistic movements in many countries of the world. Nationalism frequently provides the communists with a cloak of respectability. They "pose as the liberators of every class or nation which they intend to enslave."[12] Like nationalism, communism is a factor in the contemporary world revolution, but it is also a product of the revolution. Its rapid spread around the world could have been possible only in a revolutionary age.

Communism, which Niebuhr calls "the most dynamic and demonic world politico-religious movement in history,"[13] is an ever-present threat in many of the countries where our missionaries serve. The challenge to the missionary is greater because of the religious nature of communism—at least it serves the purpose of a religion for the communists. As Niebuhr suggests, it is a "worldwide secular religion,"[14] which tends to play "god to human history."[15] The threat to the nations of the world and to the Christian movement has been heightened by the fact that "the communist movement has managed to compound power lusts with utopian dreams in such a way as to give its totalitarian practices a dynamism and a plausibility which no one could have foreseen in this age which prides itself on its enlightenment."[16]

Missionaries face, in an unusual way, two or three problems that stem from the challenge of communism. It may be difficult for them to do it, but they should evaluate objectively the criticisms of the communists of the United States and even of organized Christianity, frankly admitting the validity of many of their accusations. Also, our missionaries must distinguish between the legitimate grievances of the masses and the propaganda of the communists who are seeking to win the masses. Missionaries must not be maneuvered into the position of opposing a better way of life for the masses—an important aspect of the contemporary revolution. Nothing would suit the communists better than to be able to lead the people to identify Christian missionaries with the privileged—with those who oppose the upward movement of the peoples of the world. On the other hand, missionaries should not become anti-communist missionaries. They go as representatives of Christ, but they should remember that the Christ they represent ministered to the needs of the sinful, sorrowing, hungry masses of mankind.

If the missionaries are to meet the challenge of communism, they must not only maintain an effective ministry to the masses, they must also perfect a strategy to reach university students. These are the two groups—the proletariat or working masses and the university students—where the communists concentrate their efforts.

DIRECTION OF THE REVOLUTION

"A sense of direction . . . is the sense of movement that is taking place under the surface of the events that make our headlines. Another name for it is a sense of history."[17] The same author also suggests that "a basic principle of statesmanship today is to determine in what direction history is moving and then to steer in that direction." This principle is as applicable to religious as it is to political statesmanship.

Some suggestions have been made previously about the direction in which the world seems to be moving in our revolutionary age. The movement is clearly toward more freedom and justice for all. This movement is related to certain trends in the economic and political areas. For example, in the economic area, the trend is toward a more equitable distribution. To accomplish this end, there is more and more control of economic processes by the political order. The direction in most areas of the world is toward a mixed economy—part free and part controlled. The only difference seems to be a matter of degree. This is even true of countries as far apart as the United States and the Soviet Union.

This should not give us undue concern. After all, economic systems, as well as political structures, are not sacred or eternal. At least, we should not be unduly concerned about the name of a system. "Names differ tremendously in their meaning and content from era to era. And, after all, there is no Christian economic system. . . . The Christian movement is concerned with the values preserved and promoted by the system rather than the name of the system. It is interested in what the system does *for* the people and *to* the people. It is not interested in labels but in achievements."[18] It is particularly important for all of us not to be frightened by "bogy words" such as "socialism," and not to label as "communistic" every new concept in the economic area.

We need something of the same perspective in the political order. While we may be strong believers in democratic government, we cannot expect the revolution in many of the new nations to express itself in democratic processes such as we have grown accustomed to in the United States. We should not expect nations that have had no experience in self-government to be democratic in terms of our interpretation of democracy. After all, we are continuing to have some problems in applying consistently our own democratic principles.

There is at least one other political trend that should be pointed out. To use Halle's expression, it represents a "sense of movement that is taking place under the surface." It is the struggle toward world unity, a struggle that goes on even under the surface of nationalistic movements. It is expressed in the political area as a movement toward some type of effective world government. Some scholars consider this to be an important aspect of the world revolution. They believe that it is one phase of the new world that is seeking to be born, and that the present period of chaos, confusion, struggle, and travail will continue until the birth takes place.

Toynbee, in a book written some years ago, said that he believed the world was going to be unified politically in the near future. He said that "the big and really formidable political issue today is, not *whether* the world is soon going to be unified politically, but in which of two alternate possible ways this rapid unification is going to come about."[19] The two ways Toynbee suggested were through the voluntary cooperation of the nations of the world or by force. The latter might result from another world war, which could leave one nation powerful enough to dominate the rest of the world.

Other writers, such as Reinhold Niebuhr, agree that the trend or movement is present but they have faced up realistically to the problems in achieving such a unified world. For example, Niebuhr some years ago said that ours is an era when "one age is dead and the other powerless to be born." He further said, "The age of absolute national sovereignty is over; but the age of international order under political instruments, powerful enough to regulate the relations of nations and to compose their competing desires, is not yet born."[20] In a typical expression, he says that "the task of building a world community is man's final necessity and possibility but also his final impossibility."[21]

It possibly should be stated that we are not attempting here to evaluate this or any other movement. Neither are we concerned primarily with the possibility or impossibility of attaining any particular order or structure. We are simply seeking to describe what seems to be beneath and behind some of the struggles in our world.

All of us should have faith to believe that in the midst of the world's struggles and suffering is our heavenly Father seeking to work out His will and while doing so He watches over His own. And, as Niebuhr says, the task of achieving world community "must be interpreted from the standpoint of a faith which understands the fragmentary and broken character of all historic achievements and yet has confidence in their meaning because it knows their completion to be in the hands of a Divine Power, whose resources are greater than those of men, and whose suffering love can overcome the corruptions of man's achievements, without negating the significance of our striving."[22]

SUMMARY AND CONCLUSION

1. The present crisis or revolution, which is worldwide in scope, is the most serious the world has known since the days of the Renaissance and Reformation.

2. The revolution or crisis is basically spiritual—it involves the integrating center composed of the basic values of different cultures and civilizations.

3. Western civilization in general and the United States in a particular way are major contributors to the revolution in other parts of the world.

4. Back of and giving some unity and direction to localized revolutions is a major world revolution.

5. There are a number of contributing factors to the *revolutions* and to *the world revolution* such as science and the march of the masses, with the latter being of particular significance for the missionary.

6. Nationalism and other contemporary movements are factors in the revolution, but they are primarily expressions of the revolution.

7. Communism, both a factor in and an evidence of the world revolution, has sought everywhere to capitalize on the revolution and to capture the leadership of the revolutions. If the West "merely tries to hold the dykes against revolution all over the world, all revolutionized states will be thrown into the arms of Russia."[23]

8. A revolutionary world, as the English historian Butterfield

says, "does not call for the kind of Christianity which in a settled world associates itself with the defense of the existing order. It calls for the other kind of Christianity, the insurgent type, which goes back to first principles and measures the present order of things against these."[24]

9. Our Christian faith can speak effectively to our revolutionary world only as it speaks both from within and apart from that world. It must be immanent in the world and yet speak to the world from a transcendent point of reference.

10. We and our missionaries, who are identified with an affluent society, must guard against the temptation, in a revolutionary world, to become defenders of the status quo that is crumbling at our feet.

11. Our missionaries must increasingly become cooperating colleagues of national leaders rather than leaders of the nationals.

12. All of us should be careful that we do not isolate ourselves from the underprivileged masses, the very ones with whom the prophets and Jesus were unusually concerned.

A PERSONAL CONCLUSION

We regret to have to say that we do not believe that the rather anemic, pallid type of religion found in most of our churches and in most of our individual lives is adequate for the kind of world in which we live. This means, among other things, that if the missionary is to meet the challenges that face him, he must not simply transport to the mission field the type of Christianity found, in the main, in our churches. He must get a personally fresh grip on the vitalities of the Christian faith. This faith must become in him the dynamite of God. He must remain open and responsive to the leadership of the Divine Spirit, recognizing that the Spirit may lead in previously untrodden paths.

In turn, we at home need to seek in every way possible to revitalize the work of God in our churches. We need to attune our spiritual ears and see if the Divine Spirit has a fresh word to speak to us in our day and through us to our revolutionary world.

Regardless of the conditions in our world and even in our churches, we can be assured that there will come a time when every knee will bow "and every tongue confess that Jesus Christ is Lord, to the glory of God the Father" (Phil. 2:10-11). There will come a time when a voice from heaven will announce: "The kingdom of the world has become the kingdom of our Lord and of his Christ, and he shall reign for ever and ever" (Rev. 11:15). Surely every one of us responds: "Come, Lord Jesus!" (Rev. 22:20).

NOTES

CHAPTER 1. THE BIBLICAL BASIS FOR SOCIAL CONCERN

[1]For material on the covenant idea in the Old Testament see Walther Eichrodt, *Theology of the Old Testament*, trans. J. A. Baker (Philadelphia: Westminster Press, 1961), the first volume of a multiple volume work which is structured entirely around the covenant concept; Meredith G. Kline, *Treaty of the Great King* (Grand Rapids: Eerdmans, 1963), relates the covenant concept to the suzerainty treaties of the ancient Near East; and George E. Mendenhall, *Law and Covenant in Israel and the Ancient Near East* (Pittsburg: The Bible Colloquim, 1955), a scholarly booklet.

[2]For a distinction between apodictic and casuistic or case law, see Eichrodt, pp. 70-71, and Mendenhall, pp. 6-7.

[3]W. Robertson Nicoll (ed.), *The Expositor's Greek Testament* (New York: George H. Doran, n.d.), IV, 325.

[4]*Ibid.*, II, 912.

[5]A. T. Robertson, *Word Pictures in the New Testament* (Nashville: Broadman Press, 1930-1933), IV, 315.

[6]*Ibid.*, IV, 137-38.

[7]*Ibid.*, VI, 225.

[8]Marvin R. Vincent. *Word Studies in the New Testament* (Grand Rapids: Eerdmans, 1946), II, 357.

[9]Brooke Foss Westcott, *The Epistles of St. John* (Grand Rapids: Eerdmans, 1957), p. 156.

[10]Nicoll, V, 192.

[11]Westcott, p. 161.

[12]Robertson, VI, 233.

[13]Nicoll, V, 193.

[14]Vincent, II, 352.

[12]Robertson, VI, 233.

[16]Nicoll, I, 340.

[17]*Ibid.*, I, 103.

[18]*Ibid.*, I, 115.

[19]G. Ernest Wright, *The Biblical Doctrine of Man in Society* (London: SCM Press, 1954), p. 129.

[20]T. W. Manson, *Ethics and the Gospel* (New York: Scribners, 1960), p. 68.

[1]John A. Mackay, *God's Order: The Ephesian Letter and the Present Time* (New York: Macmillan, 1953), p. ix.

[2]*Ibid.*, p. x.

[3]J. Scott Lidgett, *God in Christ Jesus: A Study of St. Paul's Epistle to the Ephesians* (London: Charles H. Kelly, 1915), p. 2.

[4]William Owen Carver, *The Glory of God in the Christian Calling: A Study of the Ephesian Epistle* (Nashville: Broadman Press, 1949), p. 5.

[5]*Ibid.*, p. 14.

[6]Handley C. G. Moule, *Ephesian Studies: Lessons in Faith and Walk* (New York: Fleming H. Revell, n.d.), p. 147.

[7]Carver, p. 21.

[8]Ray Summers, *Ephesians: Pattern for Christian Living* (Nashville: Broadman Press, 1960), p. vi.

[9]R. W. Dale, *The Epistle to the Ephesians* (London: Hodder & Stoughton, 1897) 10th edition, p. 341.

[10]*Ibid.*, p. 342.

[11]Carver, p. 20.

[12]*Ibid.*, p. 83.

[13]*Ibid.*, p. 10.

[14]F. F. Bruce, *The Epistle to the Ephesians: A Verse by Verse Exposition* (Westwood, N. J.: Fleming H. Revell, 1961), p. 51.

[15]S. D. F. Salmond, *The Epistle to the Ephesians in The Expositor's Greek Testament*, ed. W. R. Nicoll (New York: Doran, n.d.), III, 289.

[16]Dale, p. 198.

[17]Salmond, p. 290.

[18]Bruce, p. 52.

[19]William Barclay, *Letters to the Galatians and Ephesians* ("The Daily Study Bible"; Philadelphia: Westminster Press, 1958), p. 123.

[20]Mackay, p. 97.

[21]*Ibid.*, p. 99.

[22]Markus Barth, *The Broken Wall: A Study of the Epistle to the Ephesians* (Philadelphia: Judson Press, 1959), p. 220.

[23]Mackay, p. 99.

[24]*Ibid.*, pp. 60-61.

[25]Carver, pp. 120-21.

[26]Bruce, p. 54.

[27]Barclay, p. 136.

[28]Mackay, p. 61.

[29]A. T. Robertson, *The Epistles of Paul* in *Word Pictures in the New Testament*, IV, 526.

[30]Summers, p. 45.

[31]Mackay, p. 63.

[32]*Ibid.*

[33]Bruce, p. 88.

[34]Barclay, p. 177.
[35]Mackay, p. 188.
[36]See Colossians 3:5-14 for a parallel or similar emphasis.
[37]For additional references in Ephesians, see 2:2, 10; 4:1, 17.
[38]Carver, p. 14.

CHAPTER 3. THE CHRISTIAN AND WORLD CITIZENSHIP

The notes in this chapter do not refer to specific references or annotations. Rather, three or four books are suggested that will provide background for a better understanding of the major problems that are mentioned in the chapter.

1. World Revolution or Crisis.

Herbert Butterfield, *International Conflict in the Twentieth Century* (New York: Harper and Row, 1960). By the well-known British historian who writes from a Christian perspective. The last chapter, entitled "Christianity and Global Revolution," is a real challenge to contemporary Christianity.

Christopher Dawson, *The Movement of World Revolution* (New York: Sheed and Ward, 1959). A recognized Roman Catholic scholar examines in a particular way the revolution in the West and its relation to the revolution in Asia.

Edwin H. Rian (ed.), *Christianity and World Revolution* (New York: Harper and Row, 1963). As is usually true of an edited work, the chapters are uneven. Some areas not usually considered a part of the world revolution that are included are psychiatry and communications.

Arnold J. Toynbee, *America and the World Revolution* (New York: Oxford University Press, 1962). The world revolution stemmed from "The Shot Heard Round the World." America has deserted her own revolution. Can she rejoin it?

2. Political Unification.

David Cushman Coyle, *The United Nations and How It Works* (New York: Columbia University Press, 1965). In hard back and paper. A comprehensive source book.

Elliot R. Goodman, *The Soviet Design for a World State* (New York: Columbia University Press, 1960). Our knowledge of world government is not complete without an acquaintance with the communist's program for world control. A scholarly, thoroughly documented book.

Wallace McClure, *World Legal Order* (Chapel Hill, N. C.: University of North Carolina Press, 1960). Subtitle: "Possible Contributions of the People of the United States." Of particular interest would be Part II: "Supranational Common Law and National Constitutional Law"; and Part III: "The Legal Structure of the World Community," which is mainly a discussion of the United Nations.

Three brief books that will be helpful, from different perspectives, are: *A Constitution for the World,* published by the Center for the Study of

Democratic Institutions, and originally recommended by a committee of which Robert M. Hutchins was president or chairman; Ernest A. Gross, *The United Nations: Structure for Peace* (New York: Harper and Row, 1962), published for the Council on Foreign Relations; and Robert Theobald, *The UN and the Future* (New York: H. W. Wilson, 1963), one of the Reference Shelf Series.

3. War and Peace.

Roland H. Bainton, *Christian Attitudes Toward War and Peace* (New York: Abingdon Press, 1960). History of war and peace in the West, with emphasis on Christian attitudes and actions.

Walter Millis and James Real, *The Abolition of War* (New York: Macmillan, 1963). A product of the Center for the Study of Democratic Institutions, which was established and supported by the Fund for the Republic. The thesis is that the world has outgrown or should have outgrown the war system.

Paul Ramsey, *War and the Christian Conscience: How to Wage War Justly* (Durham, N. C.: Duke University Press, 1961). The subtitle suggests the purpose of the book: a reexamination of the just war theory.

Quincy Wright, *A Study of War* (2d ed.; Chicago: University of Chicago Press, 1965). A new edition of an old (1942) but standard book on war. An abridged edition by L. L. Wright.

4. Relation of Races.

Kyle Haselden, *The Racial Problem in Christian Perspective* (New York: Harper and Row, 1959). By the Southern born and reared editor of *The Christian Century*.

George D. Kelsey, *Racism and the Christian Understanding of Man* (New York: Scribners, 1965). Racism, a religion that negates the Christian faith. The author, a Negro, is a recognized scholar.

T. B. Maston, *The Bible and Race* (Nashville: Broadman Press, 1959). Relates basic biblical principles to race relations.

Talcott Parsons and Kenneth Clark (eds.), *The Negro in America* (Boston: Houghton-Mifflin, 1966). A factual look at the Negro in the United States. A valuable general source book.

5. Communism.

Henlee H. Barnette, *An Introduction to Communism* (Grand Rapids: Baker Book House, 1964). A brief paperback with a very helpful bibliography.

Arthur A. Cohen, *Communism of Mao Tse-Tung* (Chicago: University of Chicago Press, 1964). A needed study of the Chinese brand of communism.

J. Edgar Hoover, *Study of Communism* (New York: Holt, Rinehart, and Winston, 1963). Deals more with the practices or strategies of the communists than with their philosophy or theories.

Rodger Swearingen, *The World of Communism* (Boston: Houghton-Mifflin, 1962). Answers to one hundred questions most often asked by American high school students.

6. Secularism.

Of the older books on secularism, the following are representative:

Georgia Harkness, *The Modern Rival of Christian Faith* (New York: Abingdon-Cokesbury Press, 1952). The subtitle: "An Analysis of Secularism."

Philip Arthur Micklem, *The Secular and the Sacred* (London: Hodder & Stoughton, 1948). Traces the historical relation of the two. Nothing has been written to take its place.

Many books have been written in recent years on the contemporary impact of secularism on the Christian religion. The following are representative:

D. L. Munby, *The Idea of a Secular Society and Its Significance for Christians* (New York: Oxford University Press, 1963). Title related to T. S. Eliot's *The Idea of a Christian Society*. A running comment in many parts of the book on Eliot's book.

Leslie Newbigin, *Honest Religion for Secular Man* (Philadelphia: Westminster Press, 1966). Series of lectures by an English churchman who served as a missionary in India for over twenty years. Interprets the Gospel from a secular perspective.

Paul M. van Buren, *The Secular Meaning of the Gospel: Based on an Analysis of Its Language* (New York: Macmillan, 1963). Combines the prevalent secular interpretation of the Gospel with linguistic analysis.

7. Church and State.

Oscar Cullman, *The State in the New Testament* (New York: Scribners, 1956). The relation of Jesus to the state and teachings regarding the state in the Pauline epistles and in the Apocalypse of John.

William A. Mueller, *Church and State in Luther and Calvin* (Nashville: Broadman Press, 1954). A scholarly historical and evaluative study.

Thomas Sanders, *Protestant Concepts of Church and State* (New York: Holt, Rinehart, and Winston, 1964). Also paper by Doubleday. Reveals that beliefs regarding church and state have varied considerably.

Anson Phelps Stokes and Leo Pfeffer, *Church and State in the United States* (New York: Harper and Row, 1964). A one volume condensed edition of the standard three volume set by Stokes.

CHAPTER 4. THE CHURCH AND WORLD PROBLEMS

[1]Stephen Neill, *The Unfinished Task* (London: Lutterworth Press, 1957), p. 94.

[2]Roswell Barnes, *Under Orders* (New York: Doubleday, 1961), pp. 16-17.

[3]James M. Gustafson, *A Treasure in Earthen Vessels: The Church as a Human Community* (New York: Harper and Row, 1961).

[4]H. Richard Niebuhr, *Christ and Culture* (New York: Harper and Row, 1951).

[5]Charles Malik, *Christ and Crisis* (Grand Rapids: Eerdmans, 1962), p. 1.

[6]Butterfield, *International Conflict in the Twentieth Century*, p. 119.

[7]Henry P. van Dusen (ed.), *The Spiritual Legacy of John Foster Dulles*

(Philadelphia: Westminster Press, 1960), p. 27.

⁸*Ibid.*, p. 23.

CHAPTER 5. BIBLICAL FOUNDATIONS FOR FAMILY LIVING

¹Derrick Sherwin Bailey, *Sexual Relation in Christian Thought* (New York: Harper and Row, 1959), p. 267.

²Otto A. Piper, *The Biblical View of Sex and Marriage* (New York: Scribners, 1960), p. 21.

³Derrick Sherwin Bailey, *The Mystery of Love and Marriage* (London: SCM Press, 1952), p. 44.

⁴*Ibid.*

⁵*Ibid.*, p. 52.

⁶E. E. Neufeld, *Ancient Hebrew Marriage Laws* (New York: Longmans, Green, 1944), p. 217.

⁷*Ibid.*, p. 216.

⁸Nicoll, *Expositor's Greek Testament*, III, 79.

⁹*Ibid.*, II, 838.

¹⁰*Ibid.*, III, 365.

¹¹*Ibid.*, III, 377.

CHAPTER 6. THE FAMILY AND ITS AGING MEMBERS

¹See *Aging with a Future* (Washington, D. C.: U. S. Department of Health, Education, and Welfare, n.d.), pp. 39-40.

²*Ibid.*, p. 46.

³Edith M. Stern and Mable Ross, *You and Your Aging Parents* (New York: A. A. Wyn, 1952), p. 33.

⁴Julietta K. Arthur, *How to Help Older People* (Philadelphia: J. B. Lippincott, 1954), p. 31.

⁵Stern and Ross, p. 33.

CHAPTER 7. THE CHURCHES AND DIVORCE

¹David and Vera Mace, *Marriage: East and West* (New York: Doubleday, 1960), p. 43.

²*Ibid.*, p. 47.

³Gibson Winter, *Love and Conflict: New Patterns in Family Life* (New York: Doubleday, 1958), p. 21.

⁴For a careful analysis of the pertinent Scriptures on marriage and divorce, with particular emphasis on the one-flesh concept, see Ebbie C. Smith, "The One-Flesh Concept of Marriage: A Biblical Study" (unpublished Th.D. dissertation, Department of Christian Ethics, Southwestern Baptist Theological Seminary). Ernest White, *Marriage and the Bible* (Nashville: Broadman Press, 1965), in a careful scholarly study, devotes three chapters to divorce and remarriage.

[5]William Graham Cole, *Sex in Christianity and Psychoanalysis* (New York: Oxford University Press, 1955), p. 19.

[6]Smith, p. 189.

[7]*Ibid.*, p. 190.

[8]*Ibid.*, p. 193.

CHAPTER 8. AMERICAN CULTURE AND TRADITIONAL CONCEPTS OF MARRIAGE

[1]Christopher Dawson, *The Historic Reality of Christian Culture: A Way to the Renewal of Human Life* (New York: Harper and Row, 1960), p. 13.

[2]T. S. Eliot, *Christianity and Culture: The Idea of a Christian Society and Notes towards the Definition of Culture* (New York: Harcourt, Brace, 1949), p. 198.

[3]Paul Tillich, *Theology of Culture*, ed. Robert C. Kimball (New York: Oxford University Press, 1959), p. 51.

[4]Peter L. Berger, *The Noise of Solemn Assemblies* (Garden City, N. Y.: Doubleday, 1951), p. 138.

[5]See Winthrop Hudson, *The Great Tradition of the American Churches* (New York: Harper and Row, 1953), pp. 201-202.

[6]Samuel H. Miller, *The Dilemma of Modern Belief* (New York: Harper and Row, 1963), p. 5.

[7]Martin E. Marty, *Second Chance for American Protestants* (New York: Harper and Row, 1963), p. 91.

[8]Gibson Winter, *Love and Conflict: New Patterns in Family Life*, p. 19.

[9]Gibson Winter, *The Suburban Captivity. of the Churches: An Analysis of Protestant Responsibility in the Expanding Metropolis* (Garden City, N. Y.: Doubleday, 1961), p. 17.

[10]Dawson, p. 42.

[11]Henry Steele Commager, *The American Mind: An Interpretation of American Thought and Character Since the 1880's* (New Haven: Yale University Press, 1950), pp. 429-30.

[12]Winter, *Love and Conflict*, p. 37.

[13]*Ibid.*, p. 21.

[14]*Ibid.*, p. 40.

CHAPTER 9. BIBLICAL TEACHINGS AND RACE RELATIONS

[1]James S. Stewart, *The Life and Teachings of Jesus Christ* (London: SCM Press, 1952), p. 81.

[2]Francis J. Sheed, *Society and Sanity* (London: Sheed and Ward, 1953), p. 7.

[3]A. T. Robertson, *Word Pictures in the New Testament*, IV, 526.

[4]*Ibid.*, IV, 503.

[5]*Ibid.*, IV, 299.

[6]Frank Stagg, *The Book of Acts* (Nashville: Broadman Press, 1955), p. 124.

[1]David Soper, *Racism: A World Issue* (New York: Abingdon-Cokesbury Press, 1947), p. 15.

[2]C. G. Seligman, *Races of Africa* (3d ed.; London: Oxford University Press, 1957).

[3]Ashley Montagu, *Statement on Race* (New York: Henry Schuman, 1951), p. 13. Montagu's book is a discussion and an analysis of the Unesco statement.

[4]Calvin Kephart, *The Races of Mankind: Their Origin and Migration* (New York: Philosophical Library, 1960), pp. 75-76.

[5]Montagu, p. 25.

[6]Kephart, p. 148.

[7]Seligman, p. 113.

[8]*Ibid.*, p. 43.

[9]Herbert E. Ryle, *The Book of Genesis* (Cambridge: The University Press, 1914), p. 128.

[10]Stagg, *The Book of Acts*, p. 120.

CHAPTER 11. LAW, ORDER, AND MORALITY

[1]See Arthur L. Harding (ed.), *Origin of the Natural Law Tradition* (Dallas: Southern Methodist University Press, 1954), for a series of four lectures on the natural law. Another comparatively brief book on the natural law and the divine law is Jacques Ellul, *The Theological Foundation of Law*, trans. Marguerite Wieser (Garden City, N. Y.: Doubleday, 1960).

[2]Clarence Morris (ed.), *The Great Legal Philosophers: Selected Readings in Jurisprudence* (Philadelphia: University of Pennsylvania Press, 1959), p. 422.

[3]Arthur L. Harding (ed.), *Religious Morality and Law* (Dallas: Southern Methodist University Press, 1956), p. 36.

[4]Norman St. John-Stevas, *Life, Death, and the Law* (Bloomington, Ind.: Indiana University Press, 1961), p. 14.

[5]Paul Tillich, *Morality and Beyond* (New York: Harper and Row, 1963), p. 19.

[6]*Ibid.*, p. 20.

[7]*Ibid.*

[8]Nicholas Berdyaev, *The Destiny of Man* (3d ed.; London: Geoffrey Bles, 1948), p. 84.

[9]Carl Joachim Friedrich, *The Philosophy of Law in Historical Perspective* (2d ed.; Chicago: University of Chicago Press, 1963), p. 206.

[10]*Ibid.*, p. 214.

[11]Tillich, *Morality and Beyond*, p. 39.

[12]Reinhold Niebuhr, *The Nature and Destiny of Man* (New York: Scribners, 1943), II, 246.

¹²Paul Tillich, *Love, Power, and Justice* (New York: Oxford University Press, 1954), p. 83.
¹⁴Paul Tillich, *Morality and Beyond*, p. 39.
¹⁵Tillich, *Love, Power, and Justice*, p. 25.

CHAPTER 12. CONTEMPORARY CULTURE AND SOCIETY'S RACIAL DILEMMAS

¹Gunnar Myrdal, *An American Dilemma* (New York: Harper, 1944), I, xliii.
²*Ibid.*, I, 21.
³F. J. Sheed, *Society and Sanity*, p. 7.
⁴*Ibid.*, p. 33.
⁵T. B. Maston, *Christianity and World Issues* (New York: Macmillan, 1957), p. 95.
⁶T. B. Maston, *Segregation and Desegregation* (New York: Macmillan, 1959), p. 128.
⁷Joseph B. Mayer, *The Epistle of Saint James* (Reprinted; Grand Rapids: Zondervan, 1954), p. 79.
⁸Maston, *Segregation and Desegregation*, p. 136.
⁹Maston, *Christianity and World Issues*, p. 98.
¹⁰*Ibid.*, p. 116.

CHAPTER 13. CHURCH, STATE, AND THE CHRISTIAN ETHIC

¹W. S. Bruce, *The Ethics of the Old Testament* (Edinburgh: T. & T. Clark, 1909), p. 16.
²W. Norman Pittenger, *The Historic Faith and a Changing World* (New York: Oxford University Press, 1950), p. 83.
³Nicholas Berdyaev, *Towards a New Epoch* (London: Geoffrey Bles, 1949), p. 106.
⁴George Forell, "The State as Order of Creation," *God and Caesar*, ed. Warren A. Quanbeck (Minneapolis: Augsburg Publishing House, 1959), p. 44.
⁵Heinrich A. Rommen, *The State in Catholic Thought* (London: Herder, 1945), p. 228.
⁶John C. Bennett, *Christians and the State* (New York: Scribners, 1958), p. 38.
⁷Emil Brunner, *The Divine Imperative* (Philadelphia: Westminster Press, 1943), p. 446.
⁸Emil Brunner, *Man in Revolt*, trans. Olive Wyon (Philadelphia: Westminster Press, 1947), p. 92.
⁹T. F. Torrance, *Calvin's Doctrine of Man* (London: Lutterworth Press, 1949), p. 64.
¹⁰Walther Eichrodt, *Man in the Old Testament* (London: SCM Press, 1951), p. 30.

[11]Pittenger, p. 164.

[12]Brunner, *Man in Revolt*, p. 92.

[13]Reinhold Niebuhr, *The Children of Light and the Children of Darkness* (New York: Scribners, 1944), p. 3.

[14]Sheed, *Society and Sanity*, p. 7.

[15]Nicholas Berdyaev, *The End of Our Time*, trans. Donald Atwater (New York: Sheed and Ward, 1933), p. 80.

[16]Maston, *Christianity and World Issues*, p. 43.

[17]Reinhold Niebuhr, *The Nature and Destiny of Man*, I, 57.

[18]William E. Hocking, *The Lasting Elements of Individualism* (New Haven: Yale University Press, 1937), p. 40.

[19]A. Victor Murray, *The State and the Church in a Free Society* (Cambridge: University Press, 1958), p. 1.

[20]Berdyaev, *The Destiny of Man*, p. 57.

[21]Emil Brunner, *Justice and the Social Order* (London: Lutterworth Press, 1945), p. 78.

[22]Maston, *Christianity and World Issues*, p. 290.

[23]For a brief discussion of these concepts, see Maston, *Segregation and Desegregation*, chapter 6.

[24]Reinhold Niebuhr, *Moral Man and Immoral Society* (New York: Scribners, 1932), p. xi.

[25]*Ibid.*, p. 83.

[26]*Ibid.*, p. 75.

[27]Leslie Weatherhead, *The Will of God* (Nashville: Abingdon-Cokesbury Press, 1944).

[28]Murray, p. xi.

[29]*Ibid.*, p. 37.

[30]Reinhold Niebuhr, *Christianity and Power Politics* (New York: Scribners, 1940), p. 9.

[31]William Temple, *Thoughts in Wartime* (London: Macmillan, 1940), p. 15.

[32]*Ibid.*, p. 29.

[33]Reinhold Niebuhr, *Moral Man and Immoral Society*, p. 57.

[34]Reinhold Niebuhr, *The Nature and Destiny of Man*, II, 246.

[35]Wright, *The Biblical Doctrine of Man in Society*, p. 168.

[36]Reinhold Niebuhr, *Christianity and Power Politics*, p. 9.

CHAPTER 14. THE SECULARIST THREAT TO RELIGIOUS LIBERTY

[1]Webster's *New Collegiate Dictionary* (Springfield, Mass.: G. C. Merriam, 1956).

[2]Harkness, *The Modern Rival of Christian Faith*, p. 16.

[3]Bernard Eugene Meland, *The Realities of Faith* (New York: Oxford University Press, 1962), p. 282.

[4]Stokes, *Church and State in the United States*, I, 340.

[5]Miller, *The Dilemma of Modern Belief*, p. 5.

[6]Butterfield, *International Conflict in the Twentieth Century: A Christian View*, p. 109.

[7]Miller, p. 5.

[8]*Ibid.*, p. 75.

[9]*Ibid.*, p. 94.

[10]Micklem, *The Secular and the Sacred*, p. 185.

[11]Bennett, *Christians and the State*, p. 238.

[12]D. R. Davies, *The Sin of Our Age*, (New York: Macmillan, 1947), p. 61.

[13]Miller, p. 99.

[14]Soren Kierkegaard, *Attack upon Christendom*, trans. Walter Lowrie (Boston: Beacon Press, 1956), p. 2.

[15]David Jenkins, *Beyond Religion* (London: SCM Press, 1962), p. 94.

[16]Karl A. Olson, *Passion* (New York: Harper and Row, 1963), p. 54.

[17]William Stringfellow, *A Private and Public Faith* (Grand Rapids: Eerdmans, 1962), p. 33.

CHAPTER 15. REFLECTIONS REGARDING DEMOCRACY

[1]Ralph Barton Perry, *Puritanism and Democracy* (New York: Vanguard Press, 1944), p. 439.

[2]Henry Steele Commager, *Majority Rule and Minority Rights* (New York: Peter Smith, 1950), p. 76.

[3]Norman L. Stamps, *Why Democracies Fail* (Notre Dame, Ind.: University of Notre Dame, 1957), p. 137.

[4]John H. Hallowell, *The Moral Foundation of Democracy* (Chicago: University of Chicago Press, 1954), p. 49.

[5]*Ibid.*, p. 121.

[6]*Ibid.*, p. 122.

[7]*Ibid.*, p. 129.

[8]Reinhold Niebuhr, *The Children of Light and the Children of Darkness*, p. v.

[9]Jose Ortega y Gassett, *The Revolt of the Masses* (New York: Norton, 1932), p. 17.

[10]Hallowell, p. 129.

[11]Carl F. Becker, *Freedom and Responsibility in the American Way of Life* (New York: Alfred A. Knopf, 1945), p. 3.

CHAPTER 16. THIS REVOLUTIONARY WORLD

[1]Louis J. Halle, "The World: A Sense of History," *The New Republic*, November 7, 1964, p. 100.

[2]Eduardo Frei, "The Aims of Christian Democracy," *The Commonweal*, LXXXII, No. 3 (October 9, 1964), 66.

[3]Paul Tillich, *The World Situation* (Philadelphia: Fortress Press, 1965), p. 1. This essay was first published as a chapter in *The Christian Answer*,

edited by Henry P. Van Dusen (New York: Scribners, 1945).

[4]Halle, *The New Republic*, November 7, 1964, p. 102.

[5]Toynbee, *America and the World Revolution*, p. 159.

[6]*Ibid.*, p. 86.

[7]Frank Laubach, *Wake Up or Blow Up* (Westwood, N. J.: Fleming H. Revell, 1951), p. 28.

[8]Toynbee, p. 219.

[9]*Ibid.*, p. 151.

[10]John J. Johnson, "A New Latin American Nationalism," *The Yale Review*, LIV (Winter, 1965), 187.

[11]*Ibid.*, p. 196.

[12]Reinhold Niebuhr, *The World Crisis and American Responsibility* (New York: Association Press, 1958), p. 54. This is a series of nine essays by Niebuhr collected and edited by Ernest W. Lefever.

[13]*Ibid.*, p. 16.

[14]*Ibid.*, p. 50.

[15]*Ibid.*, p. 57.

[16]Harry R. Davis and Robert C. Good (eds.), *Reinhold Niebuhr on Politics* (New York: Scribners, 1960), p. 240.

[17]Halle, *The New Republic*, November 7, 1964, p. 102.

[18]Maston, *Christianity and World Issues*, p. 143.

[19]Arnold J. Toynbee, *Civilization on Trial* (New York: Oxford University Press, 1948), p. 127.

[20]Reinhold Niebuhr, *Discerning the Signs of the Times* (New York: Scribners, 1946), p. 40.

[21]Reinhold Niebuhr, *The Children of Light and the Children of Darkness*, p. 187.

[22]*Ibid.*, pp. 189-90.

[23]Butterfield, *International Conflict in the Twentieth Century: A Christian View*, p. 36.

[24]*Ibid.*, p. 119.

INDEX

Adoption 119, 120
Adultery 73, 102, 103, 105, 107
Africa, African 61, 63, 137, 140, 141, 171, 213, 214, 220, 221
Agape 18, 19, 53, 80, 146, 157, 158, 188
Aged, aging Chap. 6
  caring for 92-96
  needs of 88-92
  respect for 89
  statistics concerning 86
  White House Conference on 86, 87
American way of life 150, 162, 220
Anarchy 99, 183, 207
Anthropocentric 62, 191
Anthropology, anthropologist 29, 139, 142
Apodictic law (see Law, apodictic)
Aquinas, Thomas 149, 152
Aristotle 152
Artificial insemination 120
Asia 213, 214, 220
Augustine 152, 181
authoritative 119, 168, 202
authorities, governing 22, 155
authority 42, 59, 79, 120, 121, 125, 156, 177, 178, 180, 184, 191, 203 211
"Babe in Christ" 49, 132
Bailey, D. S. 73, 74, 75, 234
Bainton, Roland H. 232
Barclay, William 230, 231
Barnette, Henlee H. 232
Barth, Karl 149
Barth, Markus 31, 230
Becker, Carl F. 210, 239
Bennett, John C. 194, 237, 239
Berdyaev, Nicolas 153, 179, 182, 236, 237, 238
Berger, Peter L. 113, 235
Bible, the 13, 82, 100, 125, 132, 134, 139, 141, 178 (see Scriptures, the)
  and the covenant concept 14
  and divorce 101
  and intermarriage 143
  and male and female 77
  and the nature of God 126

and parents and children 80
and the races of mankind 138
and relation of men and women 79
and science 140
compulsory reading in schools 194
Biblical revelation 6, 28, 55, 138, 185
Birth control 119
Brother, brethren 18, 19, 20, 146
Bruce, F. F. 30, 35, 177, 230
Brunner, Emil 180, 181, 237, 238
Bureaucracy, bureaucratic 208, 209
Butterfield, Herbert 65, 192, 226, 231, 233, 239, 240
Caesar 22, 39
Caillett, Émile 63, 64, 215
Calvin, John 181
Canaan, curse of 141
Carver, W. O. 27, 28, 38, 230, 231
Casuistic laws (see Law, casuistic)
Ceremony, marriage 107, 108
Child, children of God 20, 22, 23, 49, 50, 59, 65, 128, 129, 131, 145
Christ 17, 25, 29, 33, 34, 49, 50, 64, 202 (see Jesus)
  followers of 16, 52
  indwelling 31, 53
  law of 18, 186
  lordship of 49, 59, 60
  resurrected 5, 20, 33, 59
  spirit of 48, 54
  teachings of 25, 48
  union with 5, 6, 29, 30, 31, 32, 33, 35, 37, 128, 129, 131, 133, 145, 146, 165
  work of 130-132
"Christ is the answer" 49
Christendom 43, 72
Christian, Christians 25, 30, 32, 44, 76, 78
Christian, the
  as Christ incarnate 53
  as citizen 41
"Christian," as prefix 52
Christian community (see Community, Christian)
Christian ethic (see Ethic, Christian)

241

242

245